MANAGERS MANAGING

MANAGERS MANAGING

The Workings of an Administrative System

Jane Hannaway

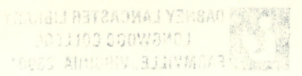

New York   Oxford
Oxford University Press
1989

Oxford University Press

Oxford New York Toronto
Delhi Bombay Calcutta Madras Karachi
Petaling Jaya Singapore Hong Kong Tokyo
Nairobi Dar es Salaam Cape Town
Melbourne Auckland

and associated companies in
Berlin Ibadan

Library of Congress Cataloging-in-Publication Data

Hannaway, Jane.
Managers managing : the workings of an administrative system /
Jane Hannaway.
p.   cm.
Bibliography: p.
Includes index.
ISBN 0-19-505207-2 (alk. paper)
1. Organizational behavior. 2. Executives. I. Title.
HD58.7.H369 1989
658.4—dc19   88-15232
                                                              CIP

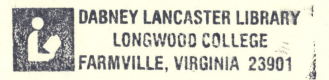
2 4 6 8 9 7 3 2 1
Printed in the United States of America
on acid-free paper

For Joe

PREFACE

This book is about what managers do on the job. What directs their behavior? Why do they do one thing and not another? These are the central questions I ask. They are beguilingly simple questions. There are over ten million managers and administrators who work in the U.S. economy, but we know little about what they actually do at work and even less about what gives them direction.

My aim is to suggest realistic interpretations of behavior in organizations. I call on the work of many different researchers to inform my analysis. I cast my net broadly. I use both field and experimental empirical results to qualify or to support the behavioral patterns that emerged in my data and I use the theoretical ideas of different disciplines — psychology, sociology, economics, and politics — to help make sense of it all. I adhere to no particular paradigm, which some readers might find frustrating. When there are alternative explanations for some behavior and I am unable to rule one of them out on the basis of empirical evidence, I offer both.

The focus of this study is on those managers who work in what I call administrative systems. They have no direct responsibility for production activities in the organization. They are located in the upper ranks of the hierarchy, responsible for strategy development and overall planning and coordination.

I offer no "quick fix" for organizational problems, although my findings have implications for making administrative systems function better, which are developed throughout the book. I likewise provide no easy solutions or prescriptions. Improving administrative systems is a complicated and tricky business. Every organization is the product of its own history, which also affects its future. Each has its own set of personalities who make things happen. Organizations are also dynamic; modifying them is like shooting a moving target with an unpredictable trajectory. Tinkering with them may be fruitful on one occasion, meaningless the next time, and disastrous at a still later date. We are not even close to possessing a complete model of organizational behavior, without it, the effects of various interventions for any particular organization at any given time are unknown.

Indeed, if solutions were simple, managers would have discovered them long ago. Most practicing managers are smart and work hard; otherwise they would not be where they are. But managers are also busy with a multitude of pressing demands. They seldom have the luxury of taking an armchair view of the workings of an organization. They may be very knowledgeable about the specific and immediate goings on of their office, but their understanding of the general nature of administrative processes that affect their own behavior and that of their colleagues is typically limited. This book gives them an opportunity to take a more detached view. It delineates some of the processes involved in administrative work and the basic behavioral patterns and problems that result from these processes. Although I discuss the implications of these processes for an organization's well-being, I would rely on the judgment of practicing managers — who know best the intimate details of their organizations — for specific solutions.

There is a sense, perhaps, in which this is a "how to" book for managers, but it is a "how to *think* about it" book, not a "how to *do* it" book. It is concerned with identifying a few basic principles according to which administrative systems function. What is the inner logic of administrative work? I assume that thoughtful managers will come to reasonable solutions on their own if they think about management problems in the right way. This book could also be viewed as a "how *not* to" book in the sense that thinking about management in the wrong way will lead to false solutions.

For students of organizations, I hope this book will suggest some ideas that can be profitably pursued, with research designed to evaluate them directly. Implicit in the conceptualization of this book is a view of managers working in a system where behavior is not well defined by a technology and where even after the fact the effects of most managerial actions are hard for the manager — as well as the organization — to assess objectively. Basic questions about how managers allocate their time under these conditions and the bases on which their performance is rewarded could generate a considerable amount of new and worthwhile research.

I do not claim to provide definitive answers to the questions I pose. This study is laced with speculation. It began as an in-depth look at the functioning of one administrative system, but when I probed into the data I had collected on what managers in that system did on the job, the data intrigued me and the book grew into something larger. The data consist of random observations, over a six-week period, of fifty-two managers at work. The data are like a set of snapshots—29,640 of them, to be exact—of managers on the job. Together they form a detailed picture of the microstructure, the inner mechanics, of an administrative system at work. The patterns these data form provided the point of departure for my speculations.

I started to ask more questions and the data sometimes provided only hints and glimmers of the answers. Rather than dismissing ideas the data only suggested, I decided to pursue them and see where they led when I coupled them with the research findings and theoretical ideas of others. My research strategy became one of hunt, peck, speculate, and then seek out corroborating evidence. I worked through the data, looking for patterns and comparisons that might provide new insights into how administrative systems work. I used the data and the ideas they suggested to tell a story—or rather a number of related stories—about the behavior of managers and the factors that affected it. The result is more an interpretive essay than a report of empirical findings.

Much has been made of the difference between public and private organizations. The system I studied in detail is the central office of a school district. School districts are public organizations in the business of providing services. Administrative systems that are part of an organization producing goods for market exchange may behave differently at some levels, although perhaps not quite so differently at others. On a number of occasions I outline specific ways in which behavior in public organizations may differ from that in market-oriented organizations. But the evidence I bring to bear suggests that the similarity in administrative systems across organizations—at least at the levels I discuss—are probably greater than the differences.

Some readers might interpret this book or portions of it as a criticism of managers, though it is not intended as such. Indeed, as I wrote it, my sympathy for managers increased. Managers generally work under highly stressful conditions, with high levels of uncertainty and little guidance. Many will never be rewarded appropriately for their contributions. I dedicate this book to those beleaguered managers in the hope that by increasing their understanding of the process of which they are a part, they will be better able to cope with the stresses and ambiguities that are an endemic part of their professional lives.

The financial and intellectual support behind this book came from many sources. Seminars at the Oxford Centre for Management Studies (now Templeton College), Educational Testing Service, the World Bank, and the Graduate School of Business and the School of Education at Stanford University proved particularly useful in helping me to formulate my ideas. The book was begun while I was a visiting scholar at Stanford's Graduate School of Business and reached completion while I was a fellow at Educational Testing Service. Comments along the way from Jim March, Leonard Sayles, Barbara Ankeny, Julie Lubetkin, and my editor, Herb Addison were especially helpful. I would like to give special thanks to Keith Baker of the U.S. Department of Education for providing the initial financial support for collecting what was at the time an unusual data set, and to Fritz Mulhauser and Gail McCall, formerly with the National Institute of Education, for providing financial and intellectual support for some of the early data analysis. Financial support from the Woodrow Wilson School of Public and International Affairs at Princeton University is also gratefully acknowledged. Most of all, I am indebted to the managers I studied for giving up some of their valuable time and for their cooperation.

Princeton, N.J.   J.H.
May 1988

CONTENTS

MANAGERS MANAGING

1

Introduction

This book attempts to gain some insight into what makes an administrative system tick. What do managers do at work? Why do they do one thing and not another? What influences how they focus their attention? Which issues and actors attract them and which do they avoid? What consequences do these factors have for how the administrative system performs its tasks?

It is not obvious what directs behavior in an administrative system. The cues for action are certainly far less clear than they are in a production system, where a reasonably well understood technology typically provides guidance and/or some discernable output gives feedback — often immediate — on the consequences of different actions. Administrative systems have very little of either; that is, they have neither a very well defined technology nor very clear indicators of effects, especially in the short run. Where do managers get direction? How is their performance evaluated?

Perhaps it would be useful to describe what I mean by an administrative system. I am using the term to refer to that part of an organization that is positioned at the top of an organization chart and typically contains at least a few levels of management. It neither produces products for external exchange nor provides services directly to clients. The administrative part of an organization is intended to carry out a number of functions for the "inside." In an ideal sense it serves the production part of the organization by acquiring resources, clearing away problems, and providing guidance so that internal production can proceed unfettered and in an efficient and effective manner. The job titles of managers in an administrative system vary enormously. They certainly include top-level management and their staffs. More generally, they include any managers who are at least one step removed from direct knowledge

1

of the production process and whose information about the precise effects of their actions on a particular outcome is tenuous, at least in the short run.

While the ideal functions of administrative systems are clear, the work itself is carried out in an environment that is complex, dynamic, and ambiguous. There are no procedures, no technologies, and no blueprints that ensure success; nor are there clear and certain connections between the actions managers take and their effects. Managers make decisions and provide guidance to organizations in a world that permits only partial understanding, where even learning by doing is limited because of ambiguous feedback. Managers are pretty much on their own, a group largely set apart, identifying issues that most need their attention, evaluating effects their earlier actions have had, and predicting effects any current actions might have in the future. In this poorly understood world, managers almost always have more issues to deal with, more things to do, more people to see, and more accessible information than they have time available. This is the nature of managerial work. There is always something additional to be learned or accomplished and no clear standards to determine when enough is enough, nor even if more (or less) would be worthwhile. New York City Mayor Ed Koch's constant query — "How'm I doin'?" — is one most managers probably often ask themselves. When I asked the question of a newly appointed state commissioner of mental health, she responded, "You never really know. Management jobs have no clear credits and debits columns with which to answer that question with much confidence." The recent rash of mass-market management books testifies to the continual search by managers for a better understanding of their complex world, or at least for a "formula" that would enable them to work effectively in that world.

How managers can best allocate their efforts is difficult to determine on a priori grounds. Indeed, it may not even be possible, given the ambiguous, complex, and dynamic nature of their environment. The process by which managers identify problems amid ambiguous stimuli, become aware of and select information from the slew of sources available, and proceed into courses of action is far less clear than has been assumed by early management theorists. The outcomes of many tasks are often hard for managers to identify; and the value of many of the identifiable outcomes often cannot be ascertained, especially in the short run. Yet, amid this ambiguity and without any clear guidelines, managers somehow allocate their time. One of the purposes of this study is to identify some of the signals that give them direction.

I began my discussion with the assumption that administrative systems are, to a large extent, characterized by ambiguity; neither clear directives for appropriate managerial behavior nor clear indicators of the effects of managerial actions are readily available. This discloses another important area of ambiguity: the quality of performance of individual managers. Without performance directives and outcome indicators, unambiguous measures of a manager's worth or contribution to the organization are not available. This, of course, is a problem for both the organization and the individual manager. The organization must make distinctions among managers so that it can dispense rewards, such as promotions, and make assignments properly. And because performance judgments affect a manager's career prospects and general well-being in the organization in significant ways, they are also important for individual managers. Most managers undoubtedly try to affect these judgments. They look out for their own reputations while simultaneously directing the affairs of the organization. I argue that both of these concerns — the business of the organization and the career interests of the manager — determine what occurs in an administrative system. Therefore, in addition to identifying signals that focus the activities of managers, I also try to identify signals that managers themselves send out to underscore their own competence.

Three themes related to these concerns run throughout the book. The first is the difficulty of distinguishing among behavior that is in the best interest of the organization, of some subunit, or of an individual manager. Economic or incentive theories of organization claim that individuals accept the organization's goals as their own if they are paid enough. They are rewarded for appropriate behavior. Such theories assume that it is possible to determine when an individual is or is not behaving in the organization's best interest. In an administrative system this may not be quite so clear-cut. The connection between an action and the objectives it is intended to serve is often not obvious.

Consider, for example, a manager who spends a considerable

amount of time collecting information about various personnel moves inside a competitor's firm or in the offices of a federal regulatory agency. Was this time well spent? Does the information have only gossip value? Will it prove useful in predicting strategic moves by the competitor or a new tack by the regulator? Or will its main value be in making the manager or the division appear knowledgeable about "what's going on" even though the information has little value for influencing organizational action? These questions aside, how can the current value of the information be assessed in any totally accurate way? It may be of critical value at some future time, but the problems of the future are not yet known and are difficult to predict.

Consider another case. A manager might call frequent meetings involving a large number of participants. While the cost of these meetings in terms of managerial time is great, the returns to the organization might make them worthwhile (though it is unclear whether the manager calling for the meetings actually does the calculations). Such gatherings might produce shared meanings, commitment, and consensus among managers and keep in-house disputes (which could be more costly than the meetings) to a minimum. They might be division meetings that increase commitment to the division's objectives at the expense of those of the organization. The meetings might be ceremonial displays whose returns go mainly to whoever called them, legitimizing his or her power and prestige, with little benefit to the organization. Distinguishing among these quite different effects is very difficult. Blatant instances of self-interested behavior by any particular individual would almost certainly be detected, but most managers are smart enough not to make their motives so obvious. The more difficult problem is detecting that fraction of managerial behavior directed at private interests that can add up to significant costs for the organization when considered collectively. Attempts to control self-interested managerial behavior, however, could easily be seriously misguided and might even lead to significant negative consequences, for reasons that I discuss in chapter 4.

A second theme in this book suggests that in the absence of guidance from either a technology or the outcomes of their actions, managers rely heavily on the social structure of the system for action cues. An individual's rank, for example, is a good indicator of how other managers will value the tasks that manager initiates. The rank of the individual associated with a particular issue signals the degree of seriousness with which other managers should attend to the issue.[1] Using rank as a signal makes good sense if, as is commonly presumed, those in the upper ranks are better able — perhaps because of more experience — to determine what actions should be taken.

But managers may rely on rank for behavioral cues for reasons other than the expertise of the superior. One reason relates to the first theme about private returns. Superiors typically control the allocation of rewards in an organization. Pandering to the boss might increase the likelihood of receiving some of these "good things." Another reason is that rank provides a simple and clear rule for sorting tasks. If managers behave in ways that simplify their complex worlds — or, as Simon (1957) put it, in ways that conserve cognitive effort — sorting tasks according to the rank of their carriers is an easy way of doing it. The extent to which these latter two reasons explain why managers take tasks associated with superiors very seriously creates problems for the organization. Issues emanating from the top might get more attention than they are worth to the organization, while important issues carried by lower-ranked managers might fall on deaf ears.

The third theme concerns indicators of a manager's performance. Objective measures derived from the output of the work itself are often hard to discern. As a consequence, other signals — particularly feedback from other actors — are used. These social channels, however, tend to be biased. They are more likely to carry negative information (i.e., information about "mistakes") than positive information (i.e., information about competence or success). In this sense managers work in a hostile environment.

The hostility of the environment has a number of important implications. For example, it encourages managers to behave in ways that avoid risks and protect them from the consequences of downside events. This not only discourages innovative behavior; but also suggests that managers spend a great deal of time making sure they are personally covered. Both these consequences can be very costly for the organization. For example, one manager told me that he never went out on a limb alone. Even when faced with relatively minor decisions, he made sure others concurred, or could be viewed as concurring, with his actions. As a common practice he wrote follow-up memos after meeting with other managers containing phrases such as "as we discussed yesterday" in order to share responsibility. Using this protective strategy is quite common. In the Iranscam hearings, John Poindexter used the old expression "CYA (cover your a— —) memos" to refer to such communications.

Some Antecedents

This book follows a small but solid tradition of behavioral studies of managers, including those by Stewart (1967), Cohen and March (1974), and Mintzberg (1973). Each of these studies collected and analyzed detailed records of how individual managers spent their time at work. For example, Mintzberg studied chief executive officers, Cohen and March studied college presidents, and Stewart concentrated on middle-level managers.

Like its predecessors, this book is based on detailed records of individual managers. However, its focus is different in two ways. The earlier studies analyzed the behavior of a single type of manager in different organizations, whereas this study includes nearly all the managerial-level personnel in a system, thereby providing a picture of the workings of the system as a whole. This comprehensive view allows an exploration of questions that earlier studies were unable to address. Specifically, it allows an examination of the patterns of interaction and work flow within the system and a comparison of the behavior of managers working in the same system, but under different conditions and at different hierarchical levels. Rather than focusing on one part, my analysis is concerned with how the parts fit together, with how managers affect each other.

The dictionary definition of a system is "an assemblage or combination of things or parts forming a complex or unitary whole." In this book I report the extent to which and the ways in which administrative processes produce a system. For example, my data show the internal intensity of administrative work. Managers spend the majority of their time interacting with and responding to each other. I take particular interest in who interacts with whom and over what types of issues and how the combined actions of individuals produce the behavior of the system.

Beyond its comprehensive approach, a second way that my analysis differs from earlier behavioral studies of managers is that it takes into account subjective information that was collected from the managers simultaneously with behavioral information. Earlier researchers have interpreted managerial behavior without the benefit of knowing what was going on in managers' minds at the time. This has been a severe limitation because how managers perceive their world no doubt affects their behavior. As Simon (1985) has argued, "we must characterize the situation, not as it appears 'objectively' to the analyst, but as it appears subjectively to the actors" (p. 298). Of course, this study also differs markedly from studies that are only subjective because its main focus is on what managers actually do.

This study also has theoretical antecedents that stem from Simon's notion of "bounded rationality." Individuals have neither the time nor the cognitive capacity to respond to all stimuli simultaneously. Consequently, they are selective, and those issues that they attend to are handled sequentially. Human attention, Simon claims, is the "bottleneck" of organizational action. Although he has not identified what gets through the bottleneck, he has argued quite persuasively that the behavior of the organization is largely influenced by managerial attention patterns. This study tries to expand this line of analysis by describing the attention patterns of managers across the organization and by identifying the processes by which their attention is directed.

The work of Williamson (1964, 1975, 1985) is also related to my analysis of the behavior of administrators. Williamson's analysis is concerned with the effect of bounded rationality, small numbers exchange problems, and individual opportunism on the efficiency of market transactions and of transactions within an organization. The basic environmental and individual characteristics that he describes are similar to those that I discuss in this book. The major difference is that here I am concerned with the internal processes that these conditions give rise to, whereas Williamson is concerned with their implications for structuring transactions efficiently, for example, through market or organizational mechanisms.

I should, perhaps, underscore that this is a study of *behavior*, not a study of *decisions*. Recent work on decision making has veered sharply away from a view of the decision-making process as an orderly rational one that involves first gathering relevant information, then laying out alternatives and their outcomes, and finally calculating which alternative produces the best results given the objective. It is now recognized, for example, that much of the information collected by managers has no immediate relevance to decision making; that managerial objectives are usually multiple, often conflicting, and dependent on the context; and that habits, deadlines, and the organization's social structure, participation patterns, and competing claims for attention have direct effects on choices. A clear distinction is now made in the literature between decision products and the decision-making process. The former can often be clearly identified and their effects examined; the latter is a very messy "sequence of behavior . . . that stretches back into a murky past and forward into a murkier future" (Burns, 1978; 379). It involves a number of individuals and their many separate actions, experiences, objectives, stores of information, and opinions. Rather than analyzing decisions themselves, a study of managerial behavior looks at the *processes* by which many of the premises upon which decisions are based are formed. It is a study of what managers attend to. For example, an examination of the levels and types of interaction activities that take place among managers shows the information exchange patterns through which managers form their views of the world.

Overview

Each of the remaining eight chapters of this book is devoted to a different aspect of the subject. Chapter 2 is a theoretical discussion of the nature of administrative systems. The literature it calls upon will be familiar to students of organizations. The different ways administrative systems have been viewed in the literature are discussed and the implicit assumptions in these views are pointed out.

Chapter 3 discusses the research approaches that I used and that others have used to study administrative work. While issues of research methodology could have been relegated in full to an appendix for reference by researchers, I have included some of the discussion in the body of the book because I think it is important for the general reader for three reasons. First, our current theoretical understanding of administrative systems has been stunted by the lack of a good description of managerial behavior (Simon 1955; Koopmans 1957; Williamson 1985). This chapter discusses the techniques researchers have traditionally used, the assumptions implicit in their methods, and their limitations. Second, I describe briefly the data that I collected and the methods I used to do it. (Additional details are in the appendix.) Because the methods are not common, I explain my rationale for choosing them. I describe them early in the book so that the reader understands the elements of the data base before I present the patterns the data form and the ideas they suggest. Third, I discuss the particular types of data that I had problems collecting and the possible theoretical importance of these problems.

Chapter 4 analyzes and interprets the behavioral patterns that emerged in the administrative system I studied. Consistent with earlier behavioral studies of managers, the managers I observed interacted with others and reacted to the demands of others at fairly high rates. Indeed, I argue that the highly interactive and reactive natures of managerial work are its pivotal characteristics. I offer explanations for these behavioral patterns which, though reasonable from the point of view of individual managers, are not always functional for the organization.

Chapter 5 discusses the implications of managerial behavior patterns for the general functioning of administrative systems; in particular, it illustrates their effect on internal pressures for the expansion of administrative systems. This chapter provides an explanation of why attempts to resolve work-load pressure by hiring more managers is often counterproductive.

Chapter 6 focuses on possible biases in the search patterns of managers — how managers seek out and assess information — and in the way work flows within the system. For example, lower-level managers are less likely to interact about matters about which they are uncertain than they are about routine concerns. I suggest reasons for the patterns and their implications. I also discuss some solutions that practicing managers claim they have used successfully to counter biased work-flow patterns.

Chapter 7 describes those tasks that managers rate as being particularly important and, therefore, the tasks to which they probably pay particularly close attention. The responses show a clear hierarchical pattern. Managers consider the tasks they receive from out-

side funding agencies and from upper-level managers more important than the tasks they receive either from lower-level managers or
from the production part of the organization. If judgments about a
task's importance are strongly influenced by its carrier, then this has
some pretty clear implications for directing the behavior of participants in administrative systems. The carrier associated with an issue
has a major effect on how the system processes the tasks related to
the issue. This explains why simple symbolic actions by organizational leaders can have very real consequences in organizations.
Subordinates pay close attention to cues that superiors send
. . . whether superiors intend it or not.

Chapter 8 speculates about the effect on the workings of the
system of certain structural and environmental changes. Specifically, I consider the effect of altering the structure by changing the
proportion of upper-level managers. I also speculate about the effect on work-flow patterns of increasing demands from actors outside the organization. The final chapter ties the various strands
together, providing an overview and integration of the theoretical
ideas presented in the earlier chapters.

NOTE

1. It is probably not surprising that managers in both business and
government who have become known as great leaders or great failures
managed during times of change and high uncertainty. Such periods
present high-ranked managers with great opportunities and equally great
risks; if they have a reasonable amount of credibility, others are likely to
follow their directives with particular diligence.

2

The Nature of Administrative Systems

Administrative Systems

There is widespread agreement that management is important — witness the starting salaries of newly minted M.B.A.'s — yet it is not easy to identify just what administrative systems do, how they function, or indeed what their real value to an organization is. One basic reason these systems are difficult to analyze is that they do not produce anything in their own right that is readily measurable. They are made up entirely of managers, not production workers in the traditional sense; their function is one of making decisions and controlling or facilitating some process that is carried out by others. Some organizations, such as government agencies, could be considered totally administrative, and their output could be measured, at least in a general way, in terms of the number of clients or claims that are processed. But even in these organizations there are the claims processors, who basically are the workers, and those who oversee them, who are the administrators.

Without some reasonable definition and measurement of administrative output, the real worth of these systems is difficult to determine. What usually happens is that the administrative part of the organization is given full credit or full blame for what is produced. Firms tend to shake up an administration when profits go down and to award bonuses to managers when profits go up; school superintendents' contracts are not renewed when test scores go down and they receive raises when scores go up; football coaches are let go after a losing season and attract lucrative outside offers after a winning one. This, of course, is not completely unreasonable: after all, one might argue, the products of the organization, the process of production, and the effort that workers expend are, to a significant degree, the result of management decisions and management-designed incentive schemes. This is the commonly accepted view. However, managers who have actually tried to "run" organizations are the first to admit and to complain about their lack of control. Kanter and Stein (1979) quote a division president as saying: "In the 1960s we thought we were really terrific. We patted ourselves on the back a lot because every decision was so successful. Business kept expanding. Then came the recession, and we couldn't do anything to stop it. We had been lucky before. Everything turned to gold in the 1960s. But it became clear that we don't know the first thing about how to make this enterprise work" (p. 27). Another executive made a similar confession: "We don't know how to manage these giant structures; and I suspect no one does. They are like dinosaurs, lumbering on of their own accord, even if they are no longer functional." Managers may be particularly willing to admit their lack of control during hard times; but the fact is that we do not know how much to credit or to blame an administration for an organization's productivity, nor do we have a very good idea how to go about making such an estimate.

A dramatic example of our ignorance about the value of management is the massive restructuring currently going on in many corporations. Administrative ranks have been slashed. Nearly every major corporation has drastically slimmed down its management bulges. The individuals affected by the cuts are often incredulous. They claim they were working hard, doing things that they thought were important and believed the company thought were important. The cutbacks, they claim, were not rational. Probably not. But the reason they were not rational is not because those who made the decisions were either crazy or were out to get someone; in large part, it is because those in charge had no solid grounds for making a rational decision. How should they judge the value of those in the managerial ranks? The number of reports written? The level of effort expended? The average IQ level? The profits of these firms may have gone down, but this does not necessarily mean the contribution of these managers was negative. Profits might have gone down more if those managers had not been there. The answer is difficult to determine. The decision to hire many of the affected managers was probably made just as ignorantly as the decision to lay them off. It is highly unlikely, for example, that the chief operating officers actually estimated the expected gain to the firm's productivity when, say, a planning unit was expanded; and, when the unit was disbanded, it is just as unlikely that they calculated much more than the savings in salaries.

The magnitude of many of the hiring "errors," if indeed they were errors, testifies in a striking way to our limited understanding of management and its value. General Motor's chairman, Roger Smith, recently announced that twenty-five thousand middle managers would be taken off the payroll in 1987 and another fifteen thousand in 1988. He claims this will result in annual savings of two billion dollars, presumably pure savings: no losses are expected to result from these cutbacks, only gains. Cutbacks in administrative positions of this magnitude are hardly marginal adjustments. Some of this slack may have been carried by General Motors on purpose, for some good reasons, but it is hard to believe that any rational profit-seeking organization would knowingly carry such high levels. General Motors is no exception; the pattern is similar in major corporations across the country. Former Deputy Treasury Secretary Richard G. Darman called the American business establishment "bloated, risk-averse, inefficient and unimaginative." How much truth is there to this?

Only a few studies have actually attempted to estimate systematically the effect of management on an organization's performance. Lieberson and O'Connor (1972), for example, looked at the performance of 167 companies and found that the effect of administrators was small relative to that of the organization's industry and stable characteristics. The findings of Salancik and Pfeffer (1977) were similar: mayors accounted for less than ten percent of the variation in most city budget expenditures. But most people do not really believe the implications of these findings. In spite of the lack of hard evidence—indeed, in spite of some evidence to the contrary—the belief that the administrative part of an organization makes a significant difference to an organization's performance is strongly and generally held. It is a highly valued part of the production process. Why else would firms pay such high salaries to managers and such large fees to executive search firms?

Why Don't We Know More?

Our lack of understanding of administrative systems is, to some degree, understandable. One major reason was mentioned earlier: the difficulty associated with identifying and measuring administrative output. We do not know *where* to look for it. There are three parts to problem. The first is that management is only one of many factors that affect organizational outcomes. Separating the effect of managers from the host of other outcome determinants, among them luck and exogeneous factors over which management has little control, such as the oil crisis, is difficult. This may sound like a technical estimation problem, but it is more than that because of the very nature of managerial work.

Therein lies the second part of the problem: managerial work involves more than solving well-defined engineering problems, for example, whether to increase the heat in the blast furnace by two degrees. It includes and is actually centered on what might be considered the residual after the engineering problems have been factored out. Studies show that managers spend very little of their time engaged in making decisions about what could be considered engineering problems (Kotter 1982; Mintzberg 1973; March and Shapiro 1982). Indeed, a good deal of managerial work involves determining, in a world with very ambiguous feedback, whether there is a problem to be solved at all and, if so, what its parameters are. It involves the political aspects of organizational behavior, such as bargaining and coalition building, in a system where preferences are not necessarily stable. It also involves human relations, which because the complexities of human nature can probably never be fully understood is always surrounded by a great deal of uncertainty in terms of the nature of the problems, the appropriateness of solutions, and the determinants of outcomes. Even if we were able to ascertain that managers had some clearly measurable effect, it would be terribly difficult to sort out the extent to which each of their separate activities contributed to it. Was an organization successful because of good strategic planning? The vision of the head? Good hiring? The commitment of employees? The answer probably is "all of the above" and a healthy dose of luck.

The third part of the problem is that managers are expected to neutralize or head off problems and crises for the organization. Evidence of success is the absence of problems. But how do you measure something that does not exist? And how do you distinguish successful managers, those who effectively neutralize problems, from "good times" managers, those who go along for the ride during relatively prosperous periods?

Not only are we uncertain about *where* to look for the output of managerial work, we do not know *when* to look for it. Managers spend considerable time, for example, on acquiring information and building networks (Kotter 1982). Acquiring information is an investment, but it is a risky investment whose future return is uncertain. It might have short-run payoffs or long-run payoffs, or maybe no payoff at all. Information that has been collected or contracts that have been cultivated could make the critical difference in an important decision; but when—and if—such a situation will arise cannot usually be predicted with much certainty. Similarly, changing (or resisting changes in), say, strategy or structure, may have beneficial (or detrimental) effects, but these may not be immediately knowable, if ever. For example, who is responsible for Bank of America's problems? Were the troubles that caused the downfall of Sam Armacost actually the makings of his predecessor, A. W. Clausen? Did the troubles simply occur after a lag so that Armacost had the bad fortune of being at the helm at the wrong time? Many financial analysts would answer "yes" to these questions. But, even with hindsight, responsibility for the problems is far from clear. In fact, Bank of America selected Clausen to succeed Armacost . . .

Help from Theories Past and Present

Classical Theory

Theoretical ideas sometimes precede and sometimes follow practical knowledge. In the case of administrative theory, theoretical ideas have not only lagged behind knowledge in practice, but may have actually limited our understanding of administrative systems. This is because traditional depictions of management in the academic literature have "assumed away" what I view to be the essence of managerial work, that is, the conditions of uncertainty and ambiguity that surround administrative processes and administrative products.

Once uncertainty is assumed away a number of other assumptions follow logically. I am particularly concerned with assumptions about connections in administrative systems. By underestimating uncertainty, traditional depictions have assumed that administrative systems are tightly connected in at least three ways. First, they have assumed that the parts of the system function in a highly coordinated and closely coupled manner. Indeed, some have gone so far as to assume that the system operates as a "unitary actor." Second, traditional views have also assumed a tight connection between preferences and actions. If one's actions are known, one's preferences can be inferred and vice versa. And third, traditional theories have assumed that managers know the value of the information they bring to bear on problems; or, at least, that the information is closely tied to, or relevant, to those problems. I discuss each of these types of connections below, along with more recent theoretical thinking that questions these connections. In the final part of the chapter, I explain the particular approach I take to the study of administrative systems.

Classical organization theory assumes that the goals of the organization are unambiguous and stable and are generally agreed upon by its participants, particularly those in the upper administrative ranks. It also assumes that the means by which the goals can best be achieved are understood well enough that clear directives and incentives for productive behavior can be established and coordinated throughout the organization. Classical theory has no room for ambiguity or conflict with regard to goals and no place for uncertainty about process or outcome. The main task of management in this view is calculation and control. Managers design rules, procedures, and incentive schemes to ensure that those in the lower ranks actually do what management *knows* should be done. It is an engineering job: seeing that the dials are set correctly on various parts of the machine (i.e., that workers are performing the right tasks) and that faulty parts (unproductive workers) are weeded out.

It should probably not be surprising that, given the above assumptions, the literature has also characterized the organization anthropomorphically, with management as the brain directing the actions of its various limbs. The parts of the organization are assumed to be tightly connected, held together and controlled by a head that knows what to accomplish and how best to go about it. Economists, traditionally anyway, have subscribed to this view of the firm as a unitary actor maximizing some objective subject to constraints. Sociologists who see the organization, qua organization, as rationally adapting its structure to environmental or technological conditions implicitly take a similar view. (See Scott 1975 for a review.)

Even the employees of an organization, especially lower-ranked employees, tend to anthropomorphize it, although since they are more aware than an outsider of their own separateness, they typically refer only to "The Administration" or "Management" as if it were an individual. A visitor from another planet might easily conjure up an image of Orwell's "Big Brother" after hearing the many apparently meaningful conversations that take place in organizations about what "The Administration" or "Management" thinks, or knows, or will do, even though it is never quite clear who the administration actually is or just what it does.

Anthropomorphizing has had consequences for the most common explanations of how an administration system functions. If a system is viewed as an individual, it is expected to behave like an individual, or maybe a superhuman individual; that is, it is expected to behave rationally, or at least to have rational intentions. This view is not "wrong"; certainly, organizations are to some significant extent purposive. However, I want to stress that this view is limited. The most important limitation is that it does not provide much insight into behaviors that are other than rational. And most people readily admit that it is quite common for administrative and organizational behavior to be at odds with the rational ideal. Organizational actors, for example, continually complain about the vagaries of organizational politics and conflicts within the organization, and clients often complain about the organization's right hand not knowing what its left hand is doing. Indeed, the complaints are so common that the term "bureaucratic" itself carries negative connotations in everyday parlance, in sharp contrast to its original Weberian meaning. How does one reconcile these complaints with the view of an organization as a unified utility maximizer?

Some might argue that the only problem with a poorly functioning organization is the incentive structure. Properly designed incentive systems would direct behavior in productive ways. In fact, a vast economics literature describing optimal incentive structures in organizations has developed. While this work might provide a reasonably good description of the kind of incentive structures that affect production activities, its appropriateness for managerial systems is more limited for the reasons I identified earlier. Unlike production operations, managerial systems are systems in which (a) the system's (or unit's) output is hard to ascertain; (b) an individual's contribution to that output is even harder to assess; (c) the effects of many actions are often felt only after a considerable lag — for example, after the actor has left the job or the situation has changed; and (d) there are large elements of risk so that it is almost always impossible to determine whether the best action was taken, given what was known, or whether a better decision at the time would have been to wait and collect more information.

Recent thinking about how organizations work and how people behave in them questions the assumptions of classical theory. This thinking explicitly recognizes that uncertainty, ambiguity, and conflict are endemic to organizations. The nature of the preferences or the goals that direct behavior in an organization and the information upon which organizational actions are based have received the most attention. Specifically, researchers have questioned the extent to which preferences are consistent and stable and the extent to which actors have good knowledge about the organization's problems, alternative actions they might take, and the consequences these actions are likely to have. Their findings suggest that organizations do not operate in the simple machinelike way that classical theories assume. We cannot, for example, infer an efficient production process based on a statement of goals; nor can we assume that an organization's preferences direct behavior in an easily predictable way.

In the next two sections I describe in more detail what researchers say about the connection between an organization's goal and its behavior and also about the extent to which, and the ways in which, individuals seek out and interpret information to inform their actions. This brief review shows some of the basic underlying complexities involved in managing and some of the reasons administrative systems are difficult to control and predict. These sections of the chapter, however, may give some readers more details than they would like. Those readers may simply want to move directly to the following section, which describes the approach I take in studying an administrative system at work.

More Recent Ideas

Goals

Questions about the nature of goals, or preferences, in organizational decision making have followed three lines. The first is concerned with differences in goals across the organization; the second with the stability of preferences over time; and the third with the congruence between the private objectives of individual managers and the objectives of the organization.

Rather than seeing the organization as a unitary actor, organization theorists, especially those concerned with decision-making processes, see it as a coalition of actors, and they see decision making by such a coalition as largely a political process (March 1962; Cyert and March 1963; Pfeffer 1977, Allison and Halperin 1972; Halperin 1974). Rather than assuming a superordinate goal for the organization, they allow for imperfectly aligned and even conflicting preferences across the organization. The concern of these theorists is with preferences that actually direct behavior, that is, instrumental objectives, not general goals, such as profit maximization, that do not have clear behavioral implications. Even if all members agree that the goal of the organization is to maximize profits, they might still disagree on how to attain that goal. Simon (1964) has argued that subunits within organizations operate with different instrumental goals or, in the words of Allison (1971,176): "Where you stand depends on where you sit." The goal of a marketing department, for instance, is to sell as much of the firm's product as possible; the goal of the R & D department is to develop new ideas and new products. Members of each subunit interpret situations in terms of the specialized problems and opportunities facing their unit (Dearborn and Simon 1958). Subunits tend to disagree, for example, on the best way for the firm to allocate new resources. Because each subunit's preferences constrain the others, bargaining and compromise are necessary to produce decisions, and these decisions are therefore unlikely to represent perfectly the preference of any single social actor or single group.

The stability of preference over time has also been questioned. Standard theories of choice assume that once preferences are given and that they hold fast; as such, they have tremendous predictive power. The connection between one's objectives at t and behavior at $t+1$ is assumed to be a close one. Others have proposed a different view: preferences are not given; rather, they are discovered or clarified through experience. They grow on you. We all know that individual tastes in food, fashion, and music change or "mature" over time. It certainly happens with children. Why assume it stops when an individual reaches adulthood? (See March 1973.) It seems reasonable to imagine that individual preferences in personal and organizational life change, expand, or become refined with experience. Changes in instrumental preferences, which is what we are concerned with here, are particularly likely as a consequence of experience.

Viewed in this way, tastes are not given or stable; they are contextual, affected by the history of the individual and the way in which the individual connects the situation at hand with that history. Evidence from laboratory studies supports this view (Tversky and Kahneman 1981). Reframing a problem and thereby connecting that problem with a different set of factors can lead to "preference reversals," even though the basic elements of the problem remain essentially the same (Slovic, Fischoff, and Lichtenstein 1982).

It is also likely that the sheer mental difficulty of an individual's maintaining and then retrieving from memory complex preference structures contributes in a significant way to the expression of preference instabilities (March 1978). Some degree of preference instability probably arises in every area of human decision making, but it cannot be ignored in the dynamic and ambiguous contexts in which most managers make choices. Hazy problems come and go frequently. Each time they come they are likely to be framed differently, affected by the organization's (or unit's) situation at the time, and by the particular concerns of whoever is carrying the problem.

Indeed, recent studies of actual decision making at the organizational level have found it difficult to explain or predict organizational actions on the basis of explicit, stable, or consistent preferences (Cohen and March 1974; March and Olsen 1976; Sproull, Weiner, and

Wolf 1978). Simple preference-determined explanations for behavior become muddled by inconsistencies in the preferences of actors within the organization as well as by what appear to be inconsistencies in the preferences of individuals over time. Once preference instability is acknowledged, it follows that more insight about organizational behavior could probably come from an understanding of the determinants of change than from an identification of a set of preferences at some particular time.

A third area that has been questioned is the degree of congruence between the objectives of the organization and the private objectives of the managers. Much of economic theory has assumed perfect congruence, for example, that profit maximization for the firm is the driving motivation behind the actions of its individual members, presumably because of the incentive structure. This view first began to be seriously questioned when ownership of large enterprises became dispersed among many shareholders. As a consequence of this dispersion, owners lost effective control and managers assumed greater power (Berle and Means 1932). The interests of owners and managers presumably differ. Owners are more interested in profits and managers are more interested in growth (Baumol 1959; Marris 1964), largely, the story goes, because of the relationship between organizational size and managerial compensation (Roberts 1959). More recently, the work of some economists, particularly that of Williamson, has attempted to incorporate the private interests of managers in personal power, status, and prestige (Barnard 1962; Simon 1976; Thompson 1961) into a theory of the firm (Williamson 1964, 1975, 1985). Traditional theorists might dismiss this work on the grounds that market discipline would not allow nonmaximizing behavior, but the everyday experiences of most organizational actors would certainly support the view that private interests direct at least some fraction of managers' behavior.

Imperfect Information

The second area of research that has seriously questioned the traditional view of the way organizations operate is concerned with the amount and type of information that managers have about the problems they face, the set of solutions available to them, and the consequences of different actions. Without good information about the connection between actions and their outcomes, for example, the bases on which they supervise the operation of the organization become questionable. In the absence of good information, what directs their actions? How do they form judgments in the face of uncertainty and ambiguity?

Although some of the first questions about the informational bases of organizational behavior can be traced back to early economic theorists, Simon is probably the best known for his work on "bounded rationality" (Simon 1955). He argued that there are limits on the human capacity to process information, and therefore there are limits on human cognition. (See Simon 1979, for a survey of his work.) Because of these limits, individuals search for information in a highly selective way and operate with simplified models of the world. Decision makers tend only to "satisfice," taking the first acceptable solution to a problem rather than searching for the optimal or best alternative.

Acquiring and using limited information, of course, is not necessarily irrational behavior. A decision maker could calculate the costs and benefits of a search and proceed with it only to the point where its expected marginal costs exceed its expected marginal benefit. At least this is what the literature on the economics of information seems to argue. But this would have to be in an ideal world. In practice, how can managers calculate the benefits of what they do not yet know? This puzzle in the economics approach to information has never been satisfactorily explained — at least not to me. Theories of search need to be developed on the basis of more believable grounds.

Recent work by sociologists and psychologists has begun to identify additional factors that affect search activities. Not only do they argue that costs, time, and cognitive abilities impose informational limitations; but, more importantly, they claim that there are systematic biases in the way information is typically acquired and used. These information biases affect a wide range of human decision making, but they are particularly relevant for managerial decision making. Managers must confront a complex environment that is beyond their full understanding and take action in it. They typically do this overloaded with information and underarmed with rules about what is relevant. In such situations information biases have a field day! To simplify, there are two stages at which biases occur, either consciously or unconsciously. The first is *informational awareness and acquisition*.[1] The second stage is that of *interpretation*, when sense is made of the information that has been acquired.

Awareness is the stage at which an actor extracts for consideration particular pieces of information from a large set of possibilities. It is impossible for individuals to absorb all available information simultaneously; they must focus on one or a few things at a time. We have probably all done this consciously at a lively cocktail party when we block out the many conversations going on around us and concentrate on one person's message. We probably also do it less consciously, say, when we notice a particularly zany advertisement and ignore others.

The process of extracting information for consideration also typically involves editing it, that is, rearranging it and putting it in some order. Weick refers to this as the process of "enactment" because what one actually absorbs is "artificial rather than natural in the sense that it is laced with preferences, purposes, idiosyncratic punctuations, desires, selective perceptions, and designs" (Weick 1979, 1976). The distinction between information that is available and information that is *acquired* by individuals in organizations is critical. An important implication of this distinction is that simply increasing the amount of information available to decision makers, a commonly proposed solution to organizational problems, will not necessarily lead to better or even different decisions. A decision maker might still be cued in to the same types of information and systematically, consciously or unconsciously, exclude other types from consideration. Most individuals know they do this. For example, managers coming out of the same meeting often compare notes to see if someone "picked up" a piece of information that they missed. What "struck" one person often goes unnoticed by another. The simple fact is that information must be noticed and acquired before it can be put to use. For managers working in an information-rich environment, this is not a trivial process.

Individuals are likely to filter out some types of information more than others. For example, information that is inconsistent with an individual's set of beliefs is likely to be screened out (Steinbrunner 1974). There is also evidence that individuals avoid information that suggests undesirable outcomes (Janis and Mann 1977;

Akerlof and Dickens 1983). Specifically relevant to organizational behavior is the finding that the biasing effect of such avoidance is exaggerated in groups where like-minded individuals communicate and reinforce information that is consistent with the group's general view and suppress information that is inconsistent or that may generate group conflict (Janis 1972). This phenomenon occurs even when it is recognized that the way the problem is handled can have very serious consequences, such as the Bay of Pigs action (Janis and Mann 1977).

Sociologists have noted biases in the selection of informational sources. For example, individuals tend to seek information from other individuals who are like themselves (Homans 1950), and they are far less likely to inquire about the views of someone who is different. They interact most naturally with people who "speak the same language," people whom they trust, even when these individuals are not particularly knowledgeable about the problem (O'Reilly 1983).

Self-interest also plays a key role in directing information acquisition activities in organizations. Managers are not normally disinterested decision makers; many decisions, such as those concerning personnel or new projects and responsibilities, affect the resources, power, and prestige of a manager or a manager's unit. It is therefore not surprising that choice may, in fact, precede an information search (Mintzberg, Raisinghani, and Theoret 1976; March and Olsen 1976); that is, the objectives of the individuals may have a greater influence on the direction and extent of the search than the problem they are trying to solve (Snyder and Swann 1978).

A second stage where bias can enter the decision-making process is the stage of *interpretation*, where decision makers impute meaning to the information they have acquired. Much of the information received by managers is complex and ambiguous and is intended to represent what is inherently a dynamic environment. Yet they must make sense of it; this is the most important part of the job. Some of the ways individuals do this and form judgments is another major source of bias affecting the information basis of organizational action.

Some of the best known and perhaps most influential work in this area has been done by cognitive psychologists. Their work extends Simon's "satisficing" model where individuals, being "boundedly rational," use shortcuts and simplifications to handle complex information-processing tasks (Simon 1955). The subsequent research of these psychologists has focused on identifying the heuristics (shortcuts or "rules of thumb") that individuals use when making judgments in uncertain situations, and the biases of intuitive judgments that result. (See Kahneman, Slovic, and Tversky 1982 for survey of this research.)

One of the significant aspects of this research on judgmental heuristics is that the same processes explain both "correct" judgments, that is, judgments made rationally, and "incorrect" judgments, that is, judgments that do not conform to the prescriptions for optimal behavior. Rational models traditionally have been used both descriptively and prescriptively. Distinctions between how individuals should behave and how they actually behave were not made. Nonrational behavior was never systematically explained; it was viewed simply as an error of judgments, and individuals committing such errors were counseled to collect more information before acting or to learn Bayesian statistics. Research by experimental cognitive psychologists shows that the heuristics that individuals use to make sense of complex information often lead to accurate estimates and judgments, but these same heuristics can also lead to biases.

I do not want to include here all the findings of this research. (See Einhorn and Hogarth 1981 and Kahneman, Slovic, and Tversky 1982 for reviews.) But it might be useful to discuss "availability," one such heuristic that is particularly relevant to managers given their complex and dynamic environment. "A person is said to employ the availability heuristic whenever he estimates frequency or probability by the ease with which instances or associations come to mind" (Tversky and Kahneman 1973, 208). It is, of course, a useful device because instances of frequent events come to mind more readily than instances of less frequent events. But it is also a heuristic than can lead to obvious biases because factors other than frequency or probability, such as saliency and recency, affect how easily something is recalled (Tversky and Kahneman 1973; Nisbett and Ross 1980). An event can be salient, for example, if it is particularly colorful, surprising, distressing, or intense.

One can easily imagine a number of situations in managerial life where the use of the availability heuristic could lead to faulty judgments. For example, one might judge the likelihood of being promoted on the basis of the number of acquaintances who have received promotions without adequately taking into consideration factors that affect promotion probabilities (or friendships). Or, one could underestimate the likelihood of adverse outcomes if instances when high risk led to high gain were fresh in one's mind. Many entrepreneurs in Silicon Valley, for example, where Apple Computer moved from a garage-scale operation to a billion-dollar concern in a few short years, and where millions have been made overnight when companies have gone public, probably underestimate risk. This might explain why many young couples in this boom area live significantly above their means. They fully expect to become millionaires soon when their actual chances are, of course, very small (*New York Times* 1984). Individuals also use the availability heuristic as well as other heuristics to make sense of complex information. Sometimes these shortcuts work well; but, as discussed above, they can also lead to biased judgments. Even when subjects are trying to make the best, most objective judgment possible, they still resort to heuristics. And neither the amount at stake nor the expertise of the subjects has any appreciable effect on their use (Slovic, Fischoff, and Lichtenstein 1977).

The findings of these experimental cognitive psychologists are no doubt very important for understanding the decision-making behavior of managers, who face uncertainty all the time. But these experimental findings alone may underestimate the extent of biased judgments on the part of managers. In real-life organizations, a number of significant situational differences emerge that may heighten the likelihood of biased judgment. One major difference is that managers typically work under pressure. Experimental laboratories, in contrast, strive to be pressure-free — unless, of course, some stress factor is under investigation. Feelings of intensity or performance anxiety that are part of the "real world" and not part of the laboratory affect judgments (Isen and Hastorf 1982). Janis and Mann (1977) argue, for example, that the stress created by uncertainty about how to handle consequential matters impairs sound decision making. Under these conditions, decision makers tend to exaggerate the possible favorable consequences of a decision and minimize the unfavorable ones.

The likelihood of biased judgments may also be greater in organizational settings than in laboratory settings because the decision makers in the experiments I described were individuals; in organizations decisions are normally made through some type of group process. Making decisions collectively is, of course, a way for individuals to compensate for their own individual limitations. They turn to each other to receive help in sorting out the implications of complex and incomplete information. For this reason, and maybe also to share the responsibility for decisions, this is the way managers make most decisions. There are thus obvious advantages to group decision making, but "groups can bring out the worst as well as the best" in individuals (Janis 1972,3). Janis, for example, has described a number of foreign policy fiascoes in which the decision-making group suffered from "groupthink" and did not realistically or objectively weigh alternatives and their consequences because of a "concurrence-seeking tendency [in cohesive groups] which fosters over optimism, lack of vigilance, and sloganistic thinking . . . " (p. 13). Issues that should generate controversy are suppressed; and limited, perhaps biased, views are reinforced.

Another basic difference between laboratory and organizational decision making is that the problems given to subjects in an experiment are structured, whereas the problems that confront managers are often unstructured or not clearly defined. Research on processing information about unstructured problems in organizational settings is very limited. This is in large part because of the messy, complicated nature of these problems. Their boundaries are unclear and always changing. "[T]he ambiguity and incompleteness of problem-related information, the extent to which problems are continually defined and redefined by managers, the lack of a program for the desired outcomes, the possibility of multiperson influences, and the extended period in which a decision is made" (Ungson, Braustein, and Hall 1981,121) all contribute to the lack of structure in these problems. These same factors make them hard to study. The few studies that have been done (March and Olsen 1976; Mintzberg, Raisinghani, and Theoret 1976) suggest that searching for information in unstructured situations does not follow the linear progression suggested by rational paradigms and research on well-structured problems, that is, moving from problem, to search, to evaluation. Choice, as suggested earlier, may precede search and evaluation. In highly ambiguous situations, choice may, in fact, direct search activities.

In some senses, the problem of unstructured problems is an unstructured problem. What should managers do, and what do managers do, when they get ambiguous signals? The traditional advice given in most management textbooks is to analyze and structure "the problem" and then list and evaluate the alternative actions that could be taken. This step in the decision-making process is typically viewed as straightforward. But with ambiguous messages, how can the problem be clearly defined? Consider a simple one: a decline in demand for a product. The decline could be due to consumer saturation, a change in tastes, or a poor advertising campaign. Notice how arguments about the nature of the problem become embedded with arguments about the appropriate solution; it is unclear which is the driving force. Indeed, one could argue that a problem is not defined as a problem until it has a solution or a set of possible solutions; without a solution, it is simply defined as a constraint. Limited resources, for example, would not be viewed as "the problem" facing a firm; the shortage of certain key personnel or the improper allocation of resources would more likely be identified. These, in fact, imply solutions. What happens when a chosen solution is determined to be not feasible? Very often the definition of the problem is changed to fit a different solution. Most problems that confront managers are complex. Selecting feasible solutions is one way for managers to give shape to the primary and secondary aspects of a complex or ambiguous problem. And those solutions that get considered may be more a function of who participates in the decision-making process and the experiences they bring with them (March and Olsen 1976) than a function of some objectively defined "problem." Ambiguous situations easily jumble what many view as the proper and usual sequential stages of decision making.

When situations cannot be objectively assessed, individuals use social means to define reality. They rely heavily on cues from others to sort out their perceptions, attitudes, and beliefs (Pfeffer and Salancik 1978). At wine tastings, for example, where indicators of quality are subtle at best, individuals typically write their ratings down. Otherwise whoever speaks first or most articulately is overly influential. Judgments in ambiguous situations are typically not independently made but are a social product. Who participates and what kind of "baggage" they carry with them clearly affect what occurs. Preexisting beliefs and values are also accentuated when individuals make judgments in ambiguously defined situations (March and Olsen 1976). As a result, differences and conflict among organizational subunits can be particularly marked.

Another basic difference between the behavior in the laboratory studies I reviewed and behavior in organizations is that in organizations managers must do more than make decisions: they must take action. In fact, organizations are more concerned with the actions that follow the judgments than with the judgments themselves. But the factors that affect behavior are not necessarily the same as those that affect judgment. For example, deadlines, rituals, the norms of the organization, and competing claims on the attention and energies of an actor can intervene between a judgment and an action. The judgments that a manager *thinks* he would exercise given a particular problem with certain dimensions may be very different from the way he would *actually behave* when, say, he was dealing with the same problem while other problems were simultaneously competing for his attention.

It should be clear from the above discussion that classical theories, which view management as a well-informed and effective controller, provide inadequate insight into how administrative systems actually function. Such theories may work well for systems characterized by stable, consistent preferences and a clear understanding of and consensus about the relationships between means and ends, but they are inadequate for understanding behavior in situations characterized by uncertainty, ambiguity, and conflict. These inadequacies in classical theories apply to certain types of jobs and to certain types of organizations more than to others. In general, the more complexity and dynamism in the environment and the more ambiguity in the technology and the output of the organization, the less likely it is that the organization will behave like a rational individual. (Even *individuals* do not conform to the rational ideal under these conditions, as I discussed earlier.) An R & D firm would probably behave less like a rational individual than, say, a widget-producing firm where the objectives, the work process, and the output are clear. With the same reasoning, we would expect the administrative part of the widget-producing firm, where the production process is well understood and the firm's profit-making objective is clear, to be less affected by the above criticisms than, say, a university, where the objectives, technology, and output are all ambiguous.

The criticisms of classical views suggest that insight into how administrative systems function will be limited indeed, and probably misleading, if we assume that individual actions follow closely some global organizational goal or if we assume that judgments are based on accurate and sufficient information. We should treat these as questions, not assumptions.

A Different Approach

The approach I take in this book is different in three basic and interrelated ways from that implied by traditional views. First, it focuses on individuals in the system, not on the system as if it were an individual. Second, it focuses on process; it examines the actual behavior of organizational participants. Behavior is not inferred either from some assumed set of preferences or from some particular set of outcomes. Third, it is particularly concerned with the extent to which, and the ways in which, individuals within the system connect with each other.

Focus on the Individual

By studying individual managers who make up the system, we can understand many types of organizational actions that are inconsistent with a simple anthropomorphic model of the organization as a unitary actor. Such models might be useful for describing the behavior of certain aggregates of organizations, such as the average firm in a particular industry, but they are not very useful for providing insight into how an individual firm behaves. For this type of understanding, information about the behavior of individuals and groups within the organization is more appropriate. March and Simon (1958) asserted thirty years ago that "propositions about organizations are statements about human behavior, and imbedded in every such proposition, explicitly or implicitly, is a set of assumptions as to what properties of human beings have to be taken into account to explain their behavior in organizations" (p. 6).

Some theorists have argued even more strongly for an individualistic focus when studying the behavior of organizations. Weick

(1979), for example, argues that to understand organizations, one must understand "organizing," that is, recurrent patterns of interaction among individuals. "Whenever an organization acts . . . people act. And any assertion that organizations act can be decomposed into some set of interacts [*sic*] among individuals . . . " (p. 34). Collins (1981) makes a similar argument:

> The active agents in any sociological explanation must be microsituational. Social patterns, institutions, and organizations are only abstractions from the behavior of individuals and summaries of the distribution of different microbehaviors in time and space. These abstractions and summaries do not *do* anything; if they seem to indicate a continuous reality it is because the individuals that make them up repeat their microbehaviors many times, and if the "structures" change it is because the individuals who enact them change their microbehaviors. (p. 989)

According to Collins's view, the causal explanations for both the inertia and the dynamics of social structures lie in the conditions that motivate individuals to behave in certain ways. This implies "that the ultimate empirical validation of sociological statements depends on their microtranslation" (p. 988).[2]

I follow the lead of these theorists, to some extent, and focus on the behavior of individual managers. I do this in order to gain insight into the nature of work *within* an administrative system and into some of the systematic inefficiencies that may be associated with it. In other words, I look inside the economist's "black box," where inputs are translated into outputs, to find out how this happens. Assuming it happens efficiently, by some mysterious process, is not very helpful for those who know this is not always the case, and who want to design organizations to function better. Organizational action, however, is something more than the sum of individuals' actions. An individual's behavior is conditioned by the social context and social structure in which he functions. In an organizational context, the manager's position in the hierarchy, for example, affects his behavior.

Focus on the Process

Analyzing administrative systems by studying organizational outcomes could be very misleading because, as we have discussed, the connections between administrative behavior and some particular set of organizational results is often tenuous. Analyzing these systems in terms of the formal goals of the organization or in terms of the stated preferences of organizational participants could also be misleading. Objectives that direct the behavior of managers vary across the organization, affected by, among other things, subunit specialization. The objectives of a unit can also change with the experiences of the actors within them. In addition, actions that best serve the interests of the organization are not necessarily those that best serve the individual.

Where does this leave us? It suggests that if we want to gain insight into the nature of managerial work, we must look at it directly. We must study the process of the work itself and from that try to identify what directs and shapes its flow in an administrative system. Analyzing managerial work through its product is not possible; we do not know quite what the product is or where or when to look for it. Nor can we completely rely on its formally stated goal or even on the intentions of its actors; standard theories of organizational choice do not fit well with much of what we know about the nature of managerial work and managerial behavior. Indeed, the view taken here is that the managers themselves are process-oriented — they define their jobs as carrying out certain functions — as opposed to being goal- or output-oriented; that they have a short-term focus; and that their time and attention are primarily regulated by the demands of others and by flows within the organization. This is not to say that managers do not respond to goals, but only that their behavior cannot be analyzed in terms of organizational goals or, indeed, in terms of broader goals that an individual might state for himself. I argue, in other words, for a detailed examination of the fine microstructures of the organization. It is these that not only determine the routines that dictate the pattern of a manager's work, but also provide the short-term goals, stimuli, and rationale for those actions that are not dictated by routine.

Focus on Connections

"[O]rganizations are the largest assemblages (of interacting human beings) in our society that have anything resembling a central coordinative system" (March and Simon 1958,4). In order to capture the ways in which the system functions as a system, I give particular attention in this study to behaviors that link individuals within the organization to each other. Indeed, the specificity of the processes of influence and the formality of the control mechanisms that operate in organizations are what distinguish organizational behavior from behavior in other settings. The effect of this control has been both overestimated by simple unitary actor models and probably underestimated by those who insist on a completely individualistic focus. I concentrate specifically on the relationship between these mechanisms and the characteristics that are basic to organizations and organizational life, for example, hierarchic position, uncertainty, and performance assessment.

NOTES

1. These are two separate stages but I am grouping them together for the sake of brevity. (See Kiesler and Sproull, 1982, for a fuller discussion.)
2. See Mayhew (1980, 1981) for a rebuttal of this view.

3

On Studying Managerial Work

The literature on management is immense and popular. The *New York Times Book Review* Best Sellers list usually includes at least a few management-oriented books, and airport book stalls are full of them. Indeed, a recent *Washington Post* article reported that two of the three hardcover, nonfiction books that have sold over one million copies in the United States during this decade are management books.[1] Most of these books advise managers to behave in ways that allegedly will increase organizational productivity. They typically take one of two tacks. Some lay out rules or principles to guide managers into behaving like "economic man," making well-informed trade-offs among alternatives. The prescriptions are often beguilingly simple, telling managers, for example, to plan their work so that they can give priority to those activities with the greatest payoffs. Other books exhort managers to be humanists, reminding them that employee productivity is affected by social and psychological factors and that creating the proper "culture" is important. The flow of books on "how to be a successful manager" seems never-ending. In contrast, the part of the management literature concerned with analyzing actual behavior within an organization—what managers actually *do* at work as opposed to what consultants *think they should do*—is quite small, though instructive.

There are theoretical and practical reasons why the study of actual behavior in administrative organizations has been neglected. The theoretical reasons center on assumptions, discussed in chapter 2, that have traditionally been about the behavior of organizations. The earliest theorists of organizations, such as Weber and Taylor, did not see the administrative part of organizations as an area that needed to be analyzed separately. The job of the manager was assumed to be defined and compartmentalized in the same way as all other jobs in the organization. Managers were simply supposed to carry out their assigned duties. Those in the upper ranks were assumed to have the knowledge and expertise to determine what tasks needed to be done in the organization, and training, rules, and supervision would take care of performance and coordination problems. Economists have not traditionally focused on the administrative part of organizations either. As discussed earlier, they assumed that the firm, as a whole, behaved like a maximizing individual. With proper incentives in place, the preferences of actors within the firm were assumed to be identical with what was in the best interest of the firm, and behavior was assumed to follow preferences directly. The only problem was to structure appropriate incentives. Organizational sociologists have given separate consideration to the administrative component of organizations, but they have been more concerned with its structural dimensions, such as its relative size, than with the behavior of actors *within* it. (For a review see Scott 1975.) Differences among individuals do not matter in this kind of analysis because they are assumed to be randomly distributed (Hall 1972). In each of these fields there are noted exceptions, and more recent work has begun to question conventional approaches. But traditionally, what went on within the administrative part of an organization was not a separate area of inquiry to any significant extent.

Simple assumptions about how administrative systems work have been allowed to persist, in part, because they have not been challenged with good evidence to the contrary (Koopmans 1957; Williamson 1985). Herbert Simon noted thirty years ago: "Administrative description suffers currently from superficiality, oversimplification, lack of realism. . . . Until administrative description reaches a higher level of sophistication, there is little reason to hope that rapid progress will be made toward the identification and verification of valid administrative principles" (Simon, 1957,38). This indictment is not quite as severe today as when it was originally made, but it still has some validity. One reason is that it is very difficult to get good data on what managers actually do on the job. This difficulty is, to some degree, related to the problem of getting access to busy managers; but, perhaps more significantly, it is related to problems associated with the methodological approaches most commonly used by researchers.

Most data in the social sciences are generated in one of three ways: through surveys, in which individuals are asked what they think, what they know, or what they do; through experiments, in which behavior is observed in carefully constructed situations and through archival research, in which records kept for other purposes are analyzed. While each of these methods has value, none is particularly well suited to the study of managerial behavior for reasons that are discussed below. Readers with little interest in research methods may want to skip this discussion, but I have included it here for the general reader as well as for the researcher. The reasons that many traditional approaches do not work well for studying managers are reasons that tell us something about the nature of managerial work. The data collection techniques I used for this book were designed specifically to minimize problems associated with the more standard methods. These techniques, along with their limitations, are described briefly later in this chapter, and details are in the appendix.

Traditional Approaches

Surveys

The most common form of social research is probably the survey — asking a large number of respondents questions about a particular topic of interest. This method offers the advantage of collecting large amounts of information, usually in a standard format, in a fairly economical way. For many topics, particularly those related to attitudes and perceptions, it is an excellent source of information; but its usefulness is limited for research on managerial behavior. There are two reasons for this: one is a problem associated with managers' making retrospective estimates of how they spend their time; the other is the absence of an appropriate vocabulary to describe managerial behavior.

There is fairly good evidence that managers, even when they try to be accurate, do not give a true description of what they do (Burns 1954; Horne and Lupton 1965; Harper 1968). Surveys, it seems, provide good information on managers' perceptions of their work, but not on the work itself. Their perceptions about how they spend their time are vulnerable to biases because of characteristics of the work. Recall the discussion in chapter 2 on the nature of administrative systems. One basic characteristic of administrative work is that it is not standardized. The problems managers deal with come in all shapes and sizes, and managers have little control over their timing. Some problems are small and well-defined; others are large and amorphous. The small, well-defined problems are the easy ones to handle; managers often have enough experience with them to be able to predict their course, and standard procedures are available to deal with them. Since little judgement is required in these situations, managers are hardly needed. The latter problems, the messy ones, are more difficult and they more aptly describe the situations where managers are needed. These are often ill-defined situations where managers must confront, interpret, and act upon a continuous, unpredictable flow of tangled issues, interdependent problems, partially understood solutions, ambiguous events, and internal political actors with differing objectives. Indeed, problems and solutions are often so intertwined that they are hard to distinguish. It is a manager's job both to make sense of this world and to figure out what (if any) actions to take. There is no schedule of work to tell them what to expect, no standard problem definitions to apply to the situations they confront; and no blueprints to tell them what to do.

Studies of actual managerial behavior, which take a micro focus, show that managers behave reactively and erratically. They switch frequently from task to task, changing their focus of attention, responding to issues as they arise, and engaging overall in a large volume of tasks of short duration. Mintzberg's chief executives, for example, averaged thirty-six written and sixteen verbal contacts per day, almost every one dealing with a distinct issue (1973,31). Most of these activities were very brief, half of them lasting less than nine minutes. More recently, managers studied by Sproull showed similar patterns. During the course of a day, they engaged in fifty-eight activities with an average duration of nine minutes (Sproull 1984,15). Interruptions also seem to be a natural part of the job. Rosemary Stewart found that her 160 managers, on average, worked uninterrupted for one-half hour only nine times during the four weeks she studied them (Stewart 1967).

Think about what survey researchers are asking managers to do when they ask them how they spend their time. They are asking them to recall thousands upon thousands of different activities and unexpected interruptions, to attach an accurate time estimate to each, and then to subtotal them in various ways on command. Unless one's work is very routine and follows fairly predictable patterns, this is exceedingly difficult to do with any reasonable degree of accuracy. Days upon days of fleeting contacts and constant interruptions leave managers with little idea about "where the time went." Almost every researcher who has gone into an organization and studied actual managerial behavior on the job has noted this. And the booming business of time management consultants, who claim they can help managers marshall their time, gives evidence of this general bewilderment.

In general, the more varied, unpredictable, and dynamic the situation being studied, the more difficult it is for anyone actively dealing with it to recall accurately how he or she has spent the time. All of these elements — variety, unpredictability, and instability — characterize the situations in which managers typically work and make retrospective time estimates particularly susceptible to biases. Managers, for instance, are likely to weigh small probability events too lightly and striking events too heavily (Tversky and Kahneman 1974). Casey (1980) provides evidence that managers remember tasks they consider particularly important, such as a high-level negotiation or a crisis, more easily than the less significant day-to-day aspects of their work. After comparing managers' estimates of time allocation with their actual behavior, Burns (1954) suggested that the estimates were based on expenditures of effort more than expenditures of time.

Normative or role expectations are another source of bias in managers' estimates. Views about what they do are affected by what they think managers should do. So if managers think that they should, or that managers in general do, spend a considerable amount of time supervising subordinates or engaged in planning, they are likely to overestimate the amount of time they spend in these ways even when they may be trying to give an accurate report. (See Webb et al. 1966 for a general discussion of this.) Probably related to this tendency is a finding by Burns (1957) that managers tend to overestimate the central aspects of their jobs, such as those concerned with production activities in the organization and with accounting, and to underestimate the subsidiary or maintenance aspects of their work, such as those concerned with personnel or human relations, which can be quite time-consuming. A particular problem with surveys is what researchers refer to as a "social acceptability" bias. Respondents try to figure out what a researcher is looking for and answer questions in ways that put them in the best possible light.

In my study I also compared manager's reports of how they spent their time with the data I collected on their actual behavior.[2] Consistent with other studies, the differences between their estimates and what they actually did on the job were significant. In follow-up interviews, the managers confirmed the validity of the study results. They claimed that the work demands during the data collection period were normal and explained that the data collection process had made them more aware of how they actually spent their time. They expressed surprise at how far off their initial estimates were.

Another reason surveys have not been particularly useful for studying managerial behavior is the lack of an appropriate vocabulary for describing behavior on the job. Traditionally the acronym POSDCORB has been used for this purpose. Coined by Luther Gulick in the 1930s, it stands for Planning, Organizing, Staffing, Directing, Coordinating, Reporting, and Budgeting. This summary description of managerial work has been, unfortunately, very influential. Most management textbooks are organized around at least a subset of these descriptors (Miner 1971, 1982; Carroll and Gillen 1987), and a considerable amount of survey research, for example, much of the Ohio State Leadership Studies,[3] was designed to estimate the extent to which similar descriptors capture the jobs of different managers. But POSDCORB descriptors have been of little use to researchers who have attempted to conduct systematic studies of the actual behavior of managers (Mintzberg 1973; Carlson, 1951).

The problem with the descriptors is simple: they do not in fact describe what managers do. At best, they describe vague *objectives* for managers. Managers are hired to plan, to organize, to coordinate, etc., but these are not operational terms. Their meanings are not behaviorally anchored; they do not correspond to empirically observable events. Take planning for example. Is this a behaviorally distinct activity? Can we tell by observing a manager at work that he or she is planning? Are planning behaviors distinguishable from, say, directing or coordinating behaviors? Probably not. What we might observe is a manager in a meeting discussing a topic with a group of other managers. Planning, coordinating, and supervising might all be going on, but only in some vague and simultaneous sense, and any attempt to code or report the behaviors with the POSDCORB descriptors would be frustrating for the manager and misleading for the researcher. Good managers indeed might argue that they are *always* planning, that is, by collecting information for possible future use, or *always* coordinating, that is, by gathering and sharing ideas and information with others.

Given the biases associated with recalling and summarizing multiple events and those associated with normative expectations, the desire for social acceptability, and the use of inappropriate descriptors of behavior, it should not be surprising that even though the Ohio State Leadership Studies spanned three decades and produced a large number of books and articles, they are viewed as contributing very little to our understanding of managerial practice, primarily because they relied on surveys. (See Campbell et al. 1970, and Mintzberg 1973 for reviews.)

Laboratory Experiments

A second common research strategy in social and behavioral science is the laboratory experiment, in which a researcher manipulates a condition, say the communication pattern in a group, and then measures the effect, for example, the group's efficiency in solving a problem.[4] The only factor allowed to vary is the experimental condition. Thus, other possible explanations for the effects are controlled by the design. These controls are the greatest advantage of experimental research because they permit the establishment of a causal sequence (Aronson, Brewer, and Carlsmith 1968). But, for our purposes, the strength of an experiment is also its weakness. It constructs a simple artificial world, one in which the complexities of real life have intentionally been left out. Experimental subjects in an isolated setting confront a clearly delimited situation, and the way they deal with that particular situation is what interests the researcher. Of course, there are many aspects of human behavior that are best studied in this way, and many would argue that it frequently is the best way to conduct research. Indeed, this approach has produced findings that are important for understanding specific aspects of individual behavior relevant for managers,[5] but it is not very useful for insights that lead to a general understanding of how individuals behave in administrative systems. These systems are by definition complex, and the problems and the stimuli that confront them are ill-defined. What is of most interest is how individuals behave in ambiguous situations where multiple stimuli are competing for their attention and where the process is ongoing, not how they behave in an isolated, short-term situation where the problem is structured and the power and status differences among participants are not salient.[6] Indeed, Mintzberg (1979) has argued that a laboratory experiment "squeezes out the very thing on which the research should focus" (p. 586).

Archival Records

A third approach social scientists employ in research is the use of archival records. These are records that are produced for other than scholarly purposes, for example, voting records or the minutes of meetings. Researchers often mine these for patterns and insights, and they provide a particularly useful basis for longitudinal analysis. The primary advantage of this type of data is their "non-reactivity"; that is, the records are not confounded by the subjects' knowing that they are part of a scholarly investigation. Organizational researchers strongly recommend greater use of archival records (Webb et al. 1966; Webb and Weick 1979), but archives alone create a very incomplete picture of managerial jobs because much of the work of managers leaves no record, such as the time they spend in informal and unscheduled interactions. This does not mean that, say, the minutes of formal meetings are not useful either in their own right or as verification of data collected in other ways, but simply that they do not capture a large fraction of what managers do, and therefore they provide only a partial view of how administrative systems actually function. Indeed, I suggest later that managers talk and write about very different things, which indicate that archival records alone could also be misleading. This is partly because written records in organizations are seldom neutral. They almost always have some underlying objective beyond the simple conveyance of information, such as justification for a particular action. The underlying objective should be taken into account in any analysis of the record, but it is usually unknown to the researcher.

Behavioral Approaches

There are two research strategies that, although not without limitations, have been used fairly successfully to study managers. One is the self-recorded diary, in which individual managers record what they do, usually at specified time intervals, and the other is structured observation, where the recording is done by a researcher. These strategies have obvious advantages over surveys, experiments, and analysis of archival data. Primary among these advantages is that, because they do not depend on managers' ability to recall and summarize their activities, they avoid the sources of many of the inherent biases of the survey method. In fact, in the observation method, managers are not the reporters at all; the researcher is the reporter. These methods also do not have the limitations of experimental or archival research. Data are collected on the managers as they operate in their naturally messy habitat, and often everything the manager does is recorded. Thus, categories of work behavior are not artificially restricted by the setting nor determined by preexisting data collected for some other purpose.

The self-recorded diary method and the structured observation method each has advantages and disadvantages. For example, because managers do the reporting themselves, the diary method can accommodate a considerably larger sample than is feasible with the observation method, which requires intensive effort on the part of the researcher to collect data. Observing and recording the behavior of one manager necessitates the full attention of a researcher. This means that it would take nearly a full year for a researcher to gather data on the work of fifty managers for only one week each. It clearly is not feasible to study a whole system simultaneously using this method. Researchers would trip over each other and no doubt disrupt ongoing processes.

Although small sample size is a distinct disadvantage of the observation method, it has other advantages in terms of flexibility and intimacy. Observations are typically structured,[7] that is, each activity is timed (usually in terms of minutes); but unlike the diary method, in which the categories are set ahead of time with the help of the manager, categories can emerge during the data collection effort as the researcher becomes more familiar with the work situation. Because the researcher is necessarily on-site, it is possible also to pick up ethnographic information about the organization that can provide valuable insights for interpreting behavioral data. This method, however, generates voluminous pages of field notes, so that probably the most arduous part of conducting research with observation techniques is the process of data reduction. With some reasonable degree of reliability, the researcher must make sense of the mountain of data collected about what a manager has done. In contrast to the massive reporting that takes place with observations, Stewart (1967) has suggested that tasks of short duration are under-reported in diaries. Some observer bias associated with the observation approach is possible, but most researchers do not think it is significant. Because of the hectic and reactive nature of most managerial jobs, if the presence of an observer is felt at all, it is either soon forgotten or not compelling enough to lead to different behaviors.

Both the observation and diary methods have disadvantages that make it difficult to secure manager participation. The diary, for example, requires extensive assistance from managers. Managers typically must learn the collection techniques, assist in defining the diary categories, and then record the data themselves. And although the observation study does not burden managers with research tasks, they still must put up with someone "shadowing" them and recording their every move.

Table 3.1 lists the major structured studies of managerial behavior and describes the basic design characteristics of these studies, that is their sample size, description of subjects, method of data collection, and length of time the managers were studied. Differences in the type and number of managers included and the duration of time over which they were studied are shown.

The Methods of This Study

Three objectives guided the selection of the data collection methods I used. First, I wanted the data to go beyond other diary and observation studies and provide insight into the system as a whole. Most studies of managerial behavior have studied individual managers of

TABLE 3.1   Design Characteristics of Major Behavioral Studies

Author	Subjects	Sample Size	Time Studied	Method
Carlson (1951)	Managing directors	9	4 weeks	Self-recorded diary
Burns (1957)	Upper-level managers	76	3-5 weeks	Self-recorded diary
Horne & Lupton (1965)	Middle managers	66	1 week	Self-recorded diary
Stewart (1967)	Middle and senior managers	160	4 weeks	Self-recorded diary
Mintzberg (1973)	Chief executives	5	1 week	Structured observation
Cohen & March (1974)	College presidents	41	2 days	Diary, recorded by secretary
Sproull (1981)	Education managers	7	3-6 days	Structured observation

a particular type (e.g., Mintzberg's chief executives and Cohen and March's college presidents) operating in different organizations. These studies have been useful; but because they focused on only one isolated part of several administrative systems, they left open a number of questions about the structure and the process of work in an administrative system. To remedy this shortcoming, I included in my study nearly all of the managers working within one administrative system. The data therefore provide a picture of how the parts of the system fit together as well as how individual managers behave on the job. This picture of a system as a whole permits an exploration of a number of questions that other studies have not been able to pursue for methodological reasons. For example: To what extent are the behaviors of managers at different levels and in different divisions connected? How does the formal structure correspond to behavior patterns? To what extent is the work of the system driven by the managers themselves, by the production process, and by the external environment? Key questions I address are the strength and types of connections among managers within the system and between them and both the production part of the organization and the external world.

In addition to getting a picture of an entire system, I had two other objectives. One was to choose methods that would minimize many of the methodological problems that have compromised the validity of earlier studies. The other was to choose methods that would allow me to get a larger sample size than observation studies permit. I used multiple means of data collection, but I obtained the most significant data by randomly sampling[8] the work activities of nearly all the managers in one administrative system. I made a total of 29,640 observations, an average of 570 for each of the 52 managers studied, using devices that housed a random signal generator. These data form the primary data base of the study. (See appendix for details on the setting, managers, and data.)

Each time managers responded to a random "beep," they answered ten questions and punched their responses directly into porta-punch cards. They reported the type of task in which they were engaged (e.g., one-to-one meeting); the content focus of the task (e.g., personnel); the ideal task performer (e.g., subordinate); the program focus of the task (e.g., special education program); and the expected disposition of the task (e.g., referral to another manager). They also identified the initiator of the task, that is, the individual or class of individuals (e.g., school principals) who asked them or in some way caused them to focus their attention on the issue at hand. They were instructed to report the most proximate cause, not the original source. This was because I felt that managers would be able to identify fairly accurately who called a particular meeting or who initiated a phone call, but that they would probably not be able to report very accurately what the original impetus was behind an initiative . . . if indeed there was one particular source.

At each beep managers also answered subjective questions designed to capture task uncertainty. I was initially interested in uncertainty in the conventional sense: that is, lack of knowledge about the consequences of actions. But my attempts in a pretest to measure uncertainty directly at the task level were unsuccessful. This is theoretically important. Managers did not think that many of their tasks were geared to outcomes that they could specify in a meaningful way. They explained that the majority of their tasks were part of some greater process, part of "doing their job." Their work seemed more process-driven, than objective-directed, and therefore could not be easily divided into discrete actions for particular outcomes that required attention, reflection, and choice; it was more of a continual flow. Rather than risking serious measurement error, I then conceptualized uncertainty in terms of the amount of experience a manager had had with a particular situation (March and Simon 1958); and I measured experience by asking managers about the routineness, frequency, novelty, and importance of the task.[9]

Another question managers had difficulty answering in the pretest concerned the purpose of the task, for example, whether it was to gather information or to supervise a subordinate. Again, this question presupposes that each task has a specifiable objective known to the manager, which apparently, is not the case. As I suggested earlier, much of managerial work is process-driven. Another part of the problem is that most managerial activities have multiple functions that occur simultaneously. For example, a manager might be monitoring, supervising, and problem solving all during one exchange with a subordinate. Indeed, it may not even be clear to the manager until after the interaction just what he or she was doing. It is interesting that when Stewart (1965) experimented with different diary formats, she reported difficulty with similar questions. She noted particularly the difficulty of obtaining consistent interpretations of actions, such as "getting information," from individuals. Some managers would interpret nearly all of their work as "getting information" while others would interpret it very narrowly. These difficulties reinforce my earlier conclusions about the inappropriateness of the POSDCORB descriptors of managerial behavior.

Managers had a difficult time answering any questions that were in any way future-oriented, which is also compatible with a process-driven view of managerial behavior. For example, many of them had trouble answering the question about the "expected disposition of the task" — whether they would complete it alone, hold it, or pass it to someone else. It was the question about which they most frequently asked for clarification.

The whole notion of task completion may be alien to managerial work. One problem is that it is difficult to define the boundaries of a task, when it begins and when it ends. Does a new task begin, for example, when the topic being discussed by a manager changes? Or perhaps when the topic remains the same and an additional manager joins the discussion? And what about interruptions? How do they affect task boundaries? For example, if someone is writing a memo and is interrupted by a telephone call, is the writing that took place after the interruption a new task? Does the duration of the interruption, or the amount of elapsed time before the task is picked up again, affect the boundary definition? One can imagine a manager's being diverted from the memo for a week. When she or he resumes writing it, maybe with additional information or a slightly different perspective, is it a new task? Researchers who have conducted observation studies have interpreted the behavior of managers in terms of activities. But they have applied their definitions *after* the data were collected. For example, Mintzberg (1973) categorized his observations into activities. He "took as the start of a new activity any point at which there was a change in the basic participants and/or the medium (a meeting, a telephone call, desk work, a tour)" (p. 271). Categorizing managerial work in this way is possible after the data are collected, but imposing such boundaries would probably seem somewhat arbitrary to managers given the natural flow of their work. Defining task boundaries is further complicated if one includes the content or the issues of the task in its definition. Many issues circulate within organizations without ever being completely resolved (Cohen, March, and Olsen 1972; Cohen and March 1974; March and Olsen 1976). For all these reasons, the results of my study are usually reported in terms of the total proportion of time spent in various ways, thus avoiding drawing arbitrary boundaries around tasks or activities.

Advantages of the Beeper Method

The random signal method of data collection used in this study has three main advantages. First of all, like the self-reported diary method, it reduces perceptual biases. Instead of having to recall or summarize their behavior, managers report exactly what they are doing at the time of the random signal and thereby tend to avoid the troublesome biases associated with the retrospective nature of survey studies. They are also less likely to underreport tasks of short duration, which according to Stewart (1967) is a problem in self-recorded diary studies. (The random signal method is also less burdensome on managers than a diary. Once managers in my study became accustomed to the questions and their "beeper," it took them only about thirteen seconds to punch a description of what they were doing into the cards.)

In general, the proportion of time managers reported they spent in a particular way should be the same as the proportion of time they actually spent that way.

The techniques used in this study not only avoid biases due to retrospective summarization, but the data suggest they also minimize social acceptability biases. For example, the socially desirable response of education managers to a question about the most important aspect of their work is probably working with teachers and students on issues related to learning. This response is probably also an accurate statement of managers' values in a global sense. But when managers rated several hundred tasks as each occurred, they were *least* likely to rate tasks concerned with curriculum or with students as being "more important" than their average task. (See Figure 7.3a.)

A second major advantage of the data collection techniques used here is that subjective measures were collected from managers at the same time as behavioral information. Taken at the task level, such measures provide a more fine-grained measure of the managers' views of their work than, say, a summary rating of the extent of routineness or the level of importance of their tasks given in an interview either before or after behavioral information is collected. By collecting behavioral and subjective information simultaneously, we have some idea of what was going on in managers' minds as they were engaged in their tasks. This is a great advantage over the observation method and provides invaluable information for interpreting behavior. Collecting subjective information at the task level is particularly important if one views perceptions, and even preferences, as being dependent upon context, as was discussed in chapter 2.

In addition to minimizing perceptual biases and providing subjective measures for explaining behavior, the third advantage of the random signal method was that it allowed me to collect information simultaneously from nearly all of the managers in one system. This information not only provided a reasonable sample size for statistical purposes, but also permitted a view of interactions and work flows within the system. Such a view, of course, would not have been feasible with the observation method since an observer for each manager would have doubled the number of people in the system! And while it is certainly possible to collect simultaneous measures with the diary method, the risk of not reporting tasks of short duration could have resulted in grossly underestimating, for example, the strength of connection among managers.

A major limitation of this study is that even though nearly thirty thousand observations of work activity were collected from fifty-two managers, all the managers were from one system, and in that sense it is a case study with the usual problems of generalization. Therefore, whenever I present a major behavioral pattern that I uncovered in the data, I also produce whatever corroborating or qualifying evidence I can find from other studies.

The data also have other limitations. One is that they do not provide an in-depth contextual view of the organization, the way a long-term ethnographic study of the system would. The ways in which the organization's history and its norms affected the behavior of participants, for example, is not known. Some unstructured observations were made about the general comings and goings of the district office, but they were mainly to identify unusual occurrences that could have affected behavior during the data collection period rather than to give a cultural understanding of the system.

In a sense, the data can be viewed as providing a structural picture of an administrative system in action where structure is defined in terms of recurrent patterns of interaction and work flow among managers, between managers and the production part of the organization, and between managers and the external environment.

NOTES

1. These are *In Search of Excellence* by Thomas Peters and Robert Waterman and *Iacocca: An Autobiography* by Lee Iacocca.

2. At the beginning of the study, a subset of managers estimated the proportion of time that they spent responding to the requests or directives of particular individuals or groups. These estimates were compared with the study results, that is, how they actually spent their time.

3. See, for example, Shartle (1949), Stogdill et al. (1956), Hemphill (1959, 1960), Mahoney, Jerdee, and Carroll (1963).

4. Such an experiment was conducted by Leavitt (1951).

5. A notable example is the work of Amos Tversky and Daniel Kahneman and associates, which is cited in this book on a number of occasions.

6. See Zelditch (1969); O'Reilly and Anderson (1987); Connolly (1977).

7. There are also observational studies that are unstructured, e.g., Sayles (1964), Dalton (1959) and Wolcott (1973). These tend to be anthropological and are very useful for understanding an organization's culture, but they are less useful for analyzing the basic structural characteristics of managerial work.

8. Kelley (1964) also used random activity sampling in a study he conducted of chief executives. See also Wirdenius (1958).

9. This measure of uncertainty implicitly assumes that managers' subjective sense of uncertainty varies directly with the amount of experience they have had with a situation (March and Simon 1958) and the importance that they attach to the task (Simon 1965:59; Zimbardo 1969:86; Janis and Mann 1977:69).

4

Pivotal Behavioral
Characteristics

Virtually every study of managers' actual behavior on the job has pictured them as constantly reacting to a barrage of demands and spending a considerable amount of time interacting with others.[1] This study is no exception; the same picture emerges. There is probably now enough cumulative evidence from various studies to suggest that reacting and interacting are the pivotal behavioral characteristics of managerial work. In this chapter I present some simple descriptions of the managers in my study in terms of these characteristics, compare them to other studies, and then tread a step beyond most earlier work to speculate about the reasons behind these behaviors. The two chapters that follow this one provide more detailed descriptions of managers at work and discuss the implications of their working patterns for the general functioning of administrative systems.

The managers I studied, like most managers, were busy. Phones were always ringing; interruptions were commonplace. Managers were often in meetings, and in between they spent time doing their paperwork and catching up on "what was going on" with other managers. As implied above, other studies of managerial behavior have described similar situations. For example, after keeping detailed minute-by-minute records on what five chief executives did on the job, Mintzberg reported that "The mail . . . telephone calls . . . and meetings . . . accounted for almost every minute from the moment these men entered their offices in the morning until they departed in the evenings. A true break seldom occurred . . . the pace was unrelenting" (1973,30).

What drives the behavior of managers? What do they do so

51

busily? The data provide clues to the answers to these questions. Classical theories, captured by the POSDCORB acronym, imply that the manager knows what needs to be done, how to do it, and when it is being done well. These theories tell part of the story, but they present a very limited picture of the job of a manager. Specifically, as I discussed in chapter 2, they do not easily accommodate views of managers as coping with uncertainty and ambiguity, which are probably the most important and the least well understood aspects of managerial work; nor do they fit in an obvious way with the descriptions of managerial behavior that emerge from the data in this study.

The data create an image of the manager as demand-driven, pushed and pulled from task to task and issue to issue—not the expected image of someone in control. The data also show the manager as a very social actor, spending most of his time with others. The image of a manager sitting alone as the master planner or master calculator is an image without a basis in reality, or at least without a basis in empirical studies of managerial behavior. These two characteristics—reactive behavior and interactive behavior— come across so strikingly in every study that has analyzed the actual job behavior of managers that an understanding of them must be central to understanding the underlying patterns of managerial behavior and more generally the nature of work flows in administrative systems. In this chapter, I try to explain why these characteristics predominate in administrative work. The data do not allow formal tests of the explanations, but they do suggest plausible stories of the dynamics behind administrative systems that are compatible with much everyday understanding of how such systems work.

Reactive Behavior

Demands bombard managers throughout most of their working day. The ones I studied spent 68 percent of their time, on average, in activities to which someone else directed them. "One damn thing after another" is the way Rosemary Stewart (1967,70) reported the feelings of the managers she studied, and most managers complain about this all the time. Warren Bennis, for example, after he took office as president of the University of Cincinnati, complained that he "had become the victim of a vast, amorphous, unwitting, unconscious conspiracy to prevent [him] from doing anything" (Bennis 1979,37). (This was in spite of the fact that Bennis is a well-known authority on organizations.) One has to suspect from observing the behavior of managers that, while managers complain about being pushed and pulled, they do not put up much resistance. Pounds (1969) came to a similar view after interviewing, observing, and interrogating fifty reputedly successful managers. These managers rarely resisted spending their time in meetings or responding to requests from others regardless of whether these requests were from superiors, peers, or subordinates. In addition, the problems they worked on were not those that they themselves had identified in interviews as concerns. They were other people's problems. When Pounds asked one manager about this, the manager responded with a smile, "That's right. I don't have time to work on my problems — I'm too busy." Another manager explained, "I don't make decisions, I just work here." Occasionally the managers I studied would attempt to protect themselves from requests, for example by having them screened by their secretaries, but in general they were very open and receptive to having their attention turned to a new matter. The only exceptions seemed to be when there was a pressing deadline,[2] say when a budget report had to be delivered to the school board; but these occasions were rare.

On the surface, reactive behavior is difficult to reconcile with the simple view that a manager is the person who orchestrates the show. But behaving reactively does not necessarily mean that managers are directed by the whims of others and that they have no choice about what they do (Stewart 1982), nor does it mean that they cannot use the demands of others opportunistically (Kotter 1982). Rather, as Mintzberg (1973) has suggested, it may mean that managers simply prefer a reactive mode of behavior. Such behavior is at odds with classical theories, but behaving reactively may be the best way of behaving given the environment in which managers generally work. In fact, it may be optimal not only in terms of organizational benefits, but also in terms of the private interests of individual managers.

Organizational Benefits

If a manager's job were simply one of engineering — a matter of calculating solutions to well-defined problems — managers might not be so reactive. Even if they were uncertain about the best solutions, they would at least be able to judge the relative importance of such problems and the relevance of available information to solving them. Managers armed with knowledge of importance and relevance could take charge quite effectively. But problems do not come to managers in neat well-defined packages; problem boundaries are typically hazy and unstable. How small problems relate to something more serious is often unclear; and information that is not obviously relevant to a particular problem at one time might turn out to be quite important later as an old problem becomes clearer or as a new problem emerges. Reliably calculating the opportunity costs of different managerial actions (the opportunities foregone as a result of doing one thing rather than another) in such a world is nearly impossible. What calculus could managers use with confidence to allocate their attention under these conditions?

One approach managers might take is experimentation, taking a "stab in the dark" and looking for the effects. Some analysts claim that this is the way managers of "successful" firms behave (Peters and Waterman 1982).[3] And, indeed, it may very well be characteristic of the most successful firms — although it may also have been characteristic of a much larger pool of unsuccessful companies that did not make it. Some may have been lucky and others not. Stabs in the dark clearly entail considerable risk.

A safer way for managers to proceed, which has been shown to have at least survival value for the organization (Radner and Rothschild 1975), is for managers to wait until problems come to them, in other words to act reactively. In the absence of perfect information about the organization, its production, and its needs for the future, letting the environment structure managerial work and trusting that the system will push up for action those issues that require tending, or those areas about which more information is needed, may work better than having managers impose a strict order of priority on only the limited set of problems they might be aware of at some particular time. At least when they are working on a crisis, they know they are working on a real problem. (Needless to say, if a manager could accurately predict and prioritize problems, it would not make much sense for him to wait for the problems to come to him.)

Sensible managers continually update their priorities; what is viewed as important today may not be considered important tomorrow as new information and new problems arise. A manager's objectives and priorities change as situations change, and in this sense situations have a stronger influence on what managers do than some set of preexisting priorities. This does not mean that managers do not search out information. Quite the contrary, they are continually exploring their environment; but theirs should be viewed as largely a passive ongoing search, directed more by the events and opportunities presented by the environment than by a set of clear objectives held by managers.[4]

Responding to the demands of others has three advantages for managers trying to sort out what tasks they should tackle. One is that being reactive might reduce uncertainty for a manager in a very real sense, in that a request from another manager provides an independent assessment of the importance of some task. A manager might have his or her own sense of a task's value, but another's calling attention to it provides verification. Consequently, a manager would have more information about the value of a task when responding to another's request than when taking his or her own initiative. Tasks received from others have a second advantage in that they have already been processed to some degree, so they tend to be better defined and more suited to immediate action than tasks that a manager might initiate on his or her own on the same topic. Since most individuals are probably better at solving problems than at formulating them from ambiguous stimuli, this mode of behavior may actually be socially efficient; that is, the marginal product of the average manager, or the output of the average manager given the contribution of other managers, would be higher. A third advantage of reactive behavior is ease: it is easier to react to demands than to sort out priorities and probabilities in a dynamic and ambiguous world. Reacting to the prompting of others conserves cognitive effort and at the same time directs action.

The data give evidence that there is wisdom to reactive behavior or passive search. Managers rated tasks received from others just as highly in terms of importance[5] as tasks they initiated on their own.[6] However, while the responsiveness of managers to the demands of others is not necessarily a bad way to operate in an ambiguous environment and may, indeed, have important survival qualities for the organization, there are conditions under which it could have quite serious negative consequences for the organization. For example, if there were strong systematic biases in the way problems and information were transmitted within the organization, the organization could be easily misdirected. This problem is considered later in the book. Let it suffice here to say that behaving reactively is not an unreasonable way for managers to behave given the conditions of their world.

Private Benefits

There are other reasons for managers to behave reactively that are more related to their private interests than to the general interests of the organization. One of the primary personal objectives of managers is to avoid or reduce risk. Specifically, they do not want to be held responsible for mistakes. Of course, no one does. But I suspect the effort managers expend in this direction is greater than that expended by most other individuals. Primarily because of the way performance feedback mechanisms typically operate in administrative systems, fear of failure may be a particularly strong motivator for managers. In addition, managers know more about how to manage their own personal risks than they do about how to handle those of the organization.

Let me define what I mean by risk. I am using risk as it is used in everyday language; in other words, limiting it to "downside" risk. I am also limiting it to risk borne by the individual personally. What is risky for the organization is not necessarily risky for the individual and vice-versa. Risk is thus used to refer to the likelihood that an outcome or a situation would be considered both negative and the responsibility of a particular individual or set of individuals.

Administrative systems operate in a way that encourages managers to engage in risk-reducing behavior. Because it is nearly impossible to calculate the actual marginal contribution of a manager (or most managerial actions) to the organization's welfare, any assessment of a manager's performance or worth is heavily influenced by prior expectations and by social feedback. In an administrative system, these factors operate in a biased fashion with the result that the chances of being held responsible for a negative outcome are greater than the chances of being rewarded for a success. One reason for this bias is the way expectations for managerial performance are structured. Another reason lies in the nature of information about the outputs of an administrative system.

Expectations about the performance of managers are lopsided by the very definition of the job; that is, positive outcomes, and perhaps *only* positive outcomes, are expected to result from what they do. In general, behavior that is expected does not attract much notice; but exceptional behavior, behavior that is *un*expected, becomes the focus of attention. Cognitive psychologists refer to this property as "salience."[7] Managers are hired to run an organization, to facilitate its operation, to make it work. That is their job and the expectation is that the organization will be better off for their efforts. (In fact, the dictionary definition of manage is "to succeed in accomplishing.") Negative outcomes from managerial actions are unexpected, and therefore they draw attention; but generally competent managerial performance, because it is expected, does not. Note that this description of a manager's function distinguishes managers from entrepreneurs. Managers are expected to oversee an organization and ensure its efficiency; entrepreneurs are expected to innovate and to take risks. Expectations about the successful performance of managers and the successful performance of entrepreneurs are thus different by the very nature of their jobs.

Performance feedback is also lopsided. The incentives for consumers, clients, and/or colleagues to call attention to a managerial failing are greater than the incentives for them to call attention to a managerial achievement.[8] In the short run, anyway, there is nothing to be gained by giving praise or expressing satisfaction with a manager's work. After all, the manager is just doing his or her job. Complaints, however, may produce payoffs. For clients or consumers, complaints can result in improved future transactions or even compensation for past losses. Criticism of a colleague, perhaps in the form of "faint praise," can also yield gains; for example, it might improve the critic's relative standing in the organization by pulling the colleague (maybe a competitor for a promotion) down a peg in the eyes of other managers. Organizations are also more likely to register complaints than praise because complaints tend to be more specific. They often assign blame, and they also typically call for action. In the face of these feedback biases, the self-protective or risk-reducing behavior of managers is quite reasonable.

One might argue that managers are also able to attract attention and appropriate rewards for superior performance. Why, then, would they favor risk-reducing behavior? One answer, perhaps, is that managers are realists: distinctly superior performance is exceedingly difficult to achieve—much more difficult than reducing risk. Superior performance in an organization is performance that exceeds some target or level of aspiration that is based on the experience and past performance of the organization and other similar organizations or organizational units (Cyert and March 1963). Most organizations that survive have performed relatively well in the past, and therefore most managers find themselves in situations where expectations for their performance are relatively high already. Managers know how to limit their risks; but to beat the target, to be an exceptionally high performer, is difficult. It is usually unclear how to do so in the dramatic way necessary to get attention, given the cumulative trial-and-error experience of many who have gone before. A manager interested in gaining recognition for high performance is well advised to choose either an organization that has recently been a poor performer or a new area where learning has not yet accumulated.

Cognitive psychologists would probably not be surprised that managers behave in ways that reduce risk. There is evidence that individuals choose riskier courses only to avoid sure losses (March 1981; Tversky and Kahneman 1974).[9] Individuals also favor actions that produce certain outcomes over actions with uncertain outcomes even though the expected values of the two types of actions are identical (Kahneman and Tversky 1979). In the case of managers, the risk-reducing behaviors discussed here can protect them, with near certainty, from being considered personally liable for negative outcomes; risk-seeking behaviors, that is, attempts to perform exceptionally well, have only some chance of success.[10] From the manager's point of view it makes sense to avoid risk. "If I am sitting in a comfortable position, why should I risk it?"

Risk avoidance has been singled out as particularly problematic in the peacetime U.S. military bureaucracy. Stories are told of generals who were coming up for promotion and refused to take any actions in the weeks before the promotion boards met for fear of making a mistake. According to one Army War College professor, perverse incentives operate in the peacetime military. "Guys are motivated by fear of failure rather than seeking success. If you try something risky and it fails, you get nailed" (Alter, Abramson, and Coppola 1984,49).

In his study of the U.S. State Department, Warwick (1975) made similar observations. Like most performance appraisal systems, ratings of officers in the State Department tended to be skewed toward the favorable end of the scale. And, in truth, most officers were probably performing at a reasonably high level. Selection boards, however, had to distinguish among candidates for promotion, and so any negative comment, or "burr" as Warwick called it, in a candidate's folder carried tremendous weight. It was grounds for not promoting an officer, and a nonpromotion would eventually result in the candidate's deselection from the Foreign Service. Not surprisingly, according to Warwick, the heavy weight given negative information produced excessive caution, conformity, and risk avoidance among aspiring officers.

Risk aversion can explain both the supply and the demand side of the work flow among managers; it can explain why managers refer matters to other managers and also why managers are open to the initiatives of others. When a problem is referred to a manager, or even just brought to her or his attention, the monkey comes to rest on that manager's back. If the problem is not attended to and it erupts into or contributes to some crisis, that manager is responsible. This responsibility makes it personally very risky for the manager not to deal with the problem. One way to handle the situation, of course, is to pass the problem—the "hot potato"—on to someone else, who would also feel pressure to respond. By doing this the manager shifts the responsibility and the risk. In some situations, because of specialized areas of responsibility, it is impossible to buck the problem completely, and the manager must deal with it directly. But if the problem is important and the consequences of different actions are unclear, the manager will probably deal directly with the problem, but in consultation with someone else. This way the problem gets handled and the manager is not solely responsible for any adverse outcomes that might ensue. Because managers do not charge each other for their time, the way lawyers bill their clients, there are few restrictions on managers' using each other in this way.

In summary, managers tend to be responsive to the initiatives of others because, if they are not, an important problem that they should be attending to might go by them. They tend to refer tasks to or confer with others, not only to get help in problem solving, but also to share any risks associated with their actions; and because there are no costs to managers for using the time of others, interdependence among managers is virtually unrestricted. In general, given the feedback biases in the system, most managers quickly learn to avoid having unattended problems left in their in-boxes, and to distribute responsibility for many actions they take.

Another aspect of the reward system in administrative organizations reinforces the reactive tendencies of managers, and it provides another reason for managers to be open to information even if it is not problem-related. As mentioned earlier, administrative feedback systems are more likely to carry information on managerial mistakes than on managerial successes. Someone who has been able to "keep his nose clean" is often assumed to be competent. But is the absence of negative information sufficient to distinguish among managers? Probably not — especially if most managers have learned to be proficient "track dusters." Other bases for distinctions must be found, and these tend to be process and input measures.

One process criterion for distinguishing managers is their receptivity and responsiveness to others. Individual scores are hard to keep, so players are valued for how they play the game. Responsiveness is a signal of worth, which induces managers to be responsive, particularly to stimuli provided by those in positions to make decisions regarding resource allocation and promotions. (This is discussed further in chapter 7.) Another proxy for competence that is readily available in administrative systems is the amount of information a manager has at his command. This is, of course, a measure of input rather than output, but it is also commonly used to signal a manager's worth (March and Feldman 1981). This way of assessing managers naturally produces strong incentives for them to acquire information; and because other actors are the major carriers of information, managers are very receptive to interactions with others. Most practicing managers and supervisors of managers probably agree that evaluating managers on the basis of what they know is common practice. Being described as "on top of things" is high praise for a manager; and being viewed as "not knowing what's going on" is probably the most damning criticism. This is discussed further in the next section of this chapter on the interactive behavior of managers. The point here is simply that managers are open not only to problems and problem-related information, but also to general information, at least partly because a manager's stock of information indicates his worth.

That both the objectives of the organization and the objectives of individual managers encourage reactive behavior poses difficult efficiency problems for administrative systems. The conflict between private interests and organizational interests is one that has long been recognized by organizational analysts. In production systems it is a problem that can be fairly easily controlled by monitoring; behavior conducted in one's private interests and behavior in line with the organization's interest either can be observed directly and distinguished (e.g., chatting with other workers about the Monday night football game vs. producing widgets) or can be inferred from output (e.g., the number of widgets produced). But in administrative systems, because it is exceedingly difficult to distinguish the behaviors associated with private interests and those associated with organizational interests, it is nearly impossible to control behaviors in ways that best serve the interests of the organization. Thus, while some level of reactive behavior may benefit the organization, the levels that managers exhibit may very well be greater than that which is optimal. The next section of this chapter on the interaction behavior of managers poses a similar problem.

Interactive Behavior

Managerial work is highly interactive. Managers spend most of their time talking: they talk in meetings; they talk informally; they talk on the telephone. How many times have you tried to get a manager on the phone and gotten a response from a secretary that he or she is "in a meeting" or "in conference" or "talking to someone right now"? The managers in my study spent on average over 63 percent of their time interacting, which corroborates the findings of other researchers:

Virtually every empirical study of managerial time allocation draws attention to the great proportion of time spent in verbal communication, with estimates ranging from 57 percent of time spent in face-to-face communication by foremen (Guest, 1956) to 89 percent of episodes in verbal interaction by middle managers in a manufacturing company (Lawler, Porter and Tennenbaum, 1968). Rosemary Stewart (1967), who collected the most extensive data, found that her middle and senior managers averaged only 34 percent of their time alone, most of the rest in informal communication, and Burns (1954) found that conversation consumed 80 percent of the middle managers' time (Mintzberg, 1973,39).

In Mintzberg's study, verbal interaction accounted for 78 percent of the managers' time. More recently, Kotter (1982) found that the general managers he studied spent, on average, 76 percent of their time interacting with others. In fact, one manager spent over 90 percent of his time talking with others (p. 80).

Why do they talk so much? Some plausible answers to this question are suggested in this section. The extent to which each separate explanation accounts for interactive behavior among managers cannot be estimated, but the discussion at least suggests some of the factors that encourage this behavior, some of the ways in which managerial work may be systematically biased, and some of the difficulties associated with instituting control mechanisms.

Managerial interactions can be either *instrumentally* or *intrinsically* motivated — or both. That is, individuals may be motivated by the payoffs associated with interaction and/or they may derive intrinsic satisfaction from the learning and affiliation associated with interaction. The payoffs or rewards may be in terms of either the objectives of the organization or the private objectives of the managers, although these need not be in conflict.

Interacting for the Payoff

Much managerial interaction can be interpreted as acquisition and clarification of information. Most of the time Kotter's general managers were involved in conversation they were asking questions. He reported one manager asking "literally hundreds of questions" in a half-hour conversation (Kotter 1982,80). Indeed, information acquisition and clarification may be the primary objectives of most managers. Finding out what is going on with one's competitors, resource providers, colleagues, and subordinates is necessary for the manager to identify problems, find solutions, and supervise organizational activities.

Some interactive behavior is very circumscribed, for example when a manager seeks to deal with a particular problem such as the purchase of a data-processing system. Other interactions may be prompted by more ambiguous stimuli, such as general malaise within a particular unit, speculations about changes in federal regulations, or hunches about the tactics of a competitor. In the latter situations, a manager would probably seek out other managers to help in verifying the existence of the situation, understanding its dimensions, and deciding if it were something that should be given closer attention.

A good deal of managerial information also seems to be acquired through a much more amorphous, almost random scanning process, in which neither the payoff nor even the object of the search is well-defined. Walking down a hall, for example, I often heard one manager casually say to another, "How did the meeting go this morning?" Sometimes the response was simply, "Fine." But more often a conversation ensued in which one manager described what was interesting or important about the meeting and then this was interpreted—maybe as a potential problem that should be monitored or perhaps simply as a lead-in to another topic—by the second manager. A good part of a manager's day is spent this way. The vast majority of verbal contacts of executives in the Mintzberg study were not planned. And Kotter (1982) found that many of the things managers discuss are only remotely connected to their jobs.

In the dynamic environment in which most managers work, there are no natural limits to information acquisition. Events must be constantly defined and interpreted and then redefined and reinterpreted. Groping may be a more appropriate way to describe managerial behavior (El Sawy 1983). Sayles (1964), after studying seventy-five managers, viewed administrative behavior in a similar way: "A manager cannot afford to think in absolutes, or fixed positions, or the 'right way.' The world of the organization does not permit this type of absolutist thinking. Administration is an iterative process; the manager must constantly rethink old decisions, remake tacit and explicit agreements with external groups, and adjust the directions he has given subordinates" (p. 205).

Another reason information acquisition is continuous is that most of the information that managers collect is not "hard" or concrete information, such as the temperature in a blast furnace; it is "soft" or ambiguous information that is difficult, if not impossible, to verify with much confidence. There are at least two reasons for this. First, managers are concerned to a large extent with the prediction of future events, and these, by definition, defy precise concrete validation in the present. The moves of a competitor, the reaction of the market to a new product, or the stability of outside funding and the regulations associated with it are all examples of future events that are of critical concern to managers, but that cannot be known in the present with certainty. In the vast majority of cases there are not even enough data to make a statistical model appropriate.

A second reason most information managers exchange is "soft" is that, in addition to being concerned about the future, managers also want to find explanations for what has happened in the past; it may help them understand the present better. But explanations of past events are typically complex and multidimensional; there is always some ambiguity and room for interpretation (March and Olsen 1976). The reasons why one firm or one school or one manager was more or less successful than another are rarely indisputable, but managers seek explanations and develop interpretations in order to make sense of things and to "learn."[11]

Managers are aware that the pieces of information they receive from other managers are "soft," that they are often hunches, and that they have sometimes been placed strategically to further an individual's or unit's position. They also know that information is processed socially and that it picks up perceptual and judgmental biases along the way (Salancik and Pfeffer 1978; Pfeffer, Salancik, and Leblebici 1976). But perceptual biases are not just "noise" in the system; they carry important information about the values and objectives of organizational actors. The problem for a manager is sorting out perceptions from objective "facts." One can imagine an endless chain of information acquisition and interpretation in an organization. Information interpreted by one division is communicated to a second division, who reinterprets the information in its own terms; this information is then communicated back to the first division, who reinterprets the information in light of the interpretation given to it by the second division . . . and so it can travel endlessly. In the weeks I spent observing managers, I heard many conversations that could be labeled "reinterpretation" exchanges in which one manager would report another manager's views of a situation and ask a third manager what she or he thought of them. If it were possible to get a complete "dump" of information from each division or from each manager that would give a complete catalog of interpretations, biases, preferences, etc., this iterative process would not be necessary. But this, of course, is not possible. Consequently, managers probe each other for new interpretations as new information becomes available. An ambiguous and dynamic situation produces ambiguous information and partial understanding and the search goes on.

Some of the information managers collect undoubtedly helps them do their jobs better, but managers also collect information because there are payoffs that benefit them as individuals and not necessarily the organization. For example, information in organizations is a source of power for the individual; it is a resource that provides access to situations in which decisions are being made and influence over those decisions (Pfeffer 1981). We have known for a long time that one's position in a communication structure determines one's power in that setting. The more central the manager the more likely he or she is to be seen, and to behave, as a leader (Leavitt 1951). Indeed, much of the interaction in organizations may be viewed as horse-trading activity among managers in which managers try to increase their stock of information in order to improve or maintain positions of power for themselves or for their coalitions.

As mentioned earlier, it pays managers to collect information because the amount of information they have available signals their worth, perhaps in the same way that the number of years of schooling is used as a signal of competence in the labor market (Spence 1974). In both cases direct observation of competence is difficult, so other indicators are used. And in both cases individuals tend to overinvest (in education or in information); they learn more than is needed to do the job because the surplus has "signaling" value. One executive, who was interviewed by Leonard Sayles, described how he determined who were good managers in this way: "You can tell whether a man is really doing a good job and on top of his department by throwing an unexpected question at him about his unit. If he has the answer at his finger tips, you can rest easy because you've got a good man there" (Sayles 1964,180). The tendency of managers to overinvest in information and to process information that may be of little use to the organization is common practice in organizations. One example was given to me by an accountant in a major international computer manufacturing firm. The accountant, at the request of his boss, conducted an internal study of the accounting division to identify the reports (1) that were used, (2) that were not used, and (3) that were not currently being prepared but that might be useful. The boss read the study carefully, but the only part that interested him was the identification of reports not being produced. He had no interest in reducing the number of useless reports, which presumably would increase the efficiency of the division. He was eager to produce more, because producing more reports was clearly to his advantage. The costs to him or his division were zero; they were absorbed by the organization as a whole. There was even some chance he could benefit if someone found a report useful and praised his efforts. Producing new reports gave him additional opportunities to demonstrate the work of his division. Criticism for producing too much information was unlikely, partly because no one would know at what point too much would be too much. The possible number of users was large, and someone who did not find the reports useful would probably assume someone else did. Criticism was more likely for *not* producing information that someone needed in a crisis than for producing too much information. The story goes that the boss won easy approval to produce the new reports. In fact, he was able to hire two additional people to work on them. The willingness of his superiors to give their approval indicates both the high level of thirst in organizations for information and the difficulty of calculating its value.

Stocking information has little benefit for managers if others are unaware of it. The lucky managers are those for whom situations arise in which they can show what they know, and if such situations do not arise, they may look for or even create them. Indeed, this may explain why extensive discussions that are not particularly relevant to decision making take place in meetings. It may also be one of the reasons so many meetings are called. Among other things, meetings are forums where managers market their competence by broadcasting their information (which is also one of the reasons managers come in from the field and work in the home office).

This reasoning explains not only why managers collect more information than they need, but also why they prefer to collect information that is not commonly known. The scarcer the resource the more valuable it is, especially if it relates to a critical source of uncertainty for the organization (Crozier 1964). Being the sole source of pertinent information in a crisis can do wonders for a manager's career. In order to get proper credit, however, managers must be very selective to whom and in what forum they dispense this information; but they must share it with someone in order to get credit for it.[12]

If managers want to behave strategically and to be influential, they must know more than problem-specific information. They must know how the problem fits into the bigger picture. They need information beyond what is directly pertinent to the issues: information about the knowledge and intentions of other actors or units. And if influence depends on information, in particular on what one knows *relative* to others, then further incentives for excessive information collections are engendered. It encourages an information "rat race" within the organization.

With the exception of studies of formal management information systems, there has been little research that has focused specifically on the acquisition and transmission of information in organizations. (See O'Reilly 1983 for review.) This is, in part, because so many of the interesting questions about how information is acquired and processed in organizations have not fit into the standard views of organizational behavior and therefore have never been fully addressed. Some influential theorists, such as Herbert Simon, James March and Richard Cyert, have viewed decision making as the central function of administrative systems, and they may be right. But this view has probably led researchers to overestimate the extent to which, and the way in which, organizational behavior is connected to decision making. In more recent work, March and his colleagues have questioned this connection (March and Olsen 1976; Feldman and March 1981). In the section below, I consider non-decision-related reasons, other than private gain, that might motivate managers to interact and to collect and to transmit information.

Interacting for Pleasure

Not all interaction behavior is for payoffs; some of it is intrinsically motivated. That is, individuals interact because it gives them satisfaction or removes or ameliorates feelings that are uncomfortable. And while, on some level, these benefits might be considered "payoffs," they are outcomes that go well beyond those normally considered by analysts to be incentives. Indeed, thinking of these outcomes as payoffs pushes the rational paradigm toward a tautological extreme.

Social psychologists claim that the quest to make sense of things is basic and, given the ambiguous nature of the managerial environment, high levels of interaction among managers should be expected even in the absence of organizational incentives. Coupled with the desire for understanding is a need to evaluate one's opinions. Individuals generally prefer to verify their views with something that is concrete and objective, for example by trying a machine to see how it works. But in an administrative environment this is not usually possible. Managers can always check the current interest rates by looking in a newspaper or by calling a bank, or verify the reading level in a particular classroom by looking at standardized test scores, but the issues that are of central concern to them, such as the interest rate even one month in the future or the gains that will result from a curriculum change, cannot be objectively verified in the present. In situations such as these, managers still attempt to verify their opinions, but they use social means, turning to each other for comparisons of opinions, beliefs, and abilities (Festinger 1954). What is particularly interesting about such interaction is that it provides reassurance for the individual, not new information to be used on the job. And while new information may be acquired along the way, most interaction motivated in this way typically takes place with individuals who hold similar opinions (Festinger 1954). It is thus often a way of "bolstering" opinion (Janis and Mann 1977; O'Reilly 1983), rather than searching out information.

A similar line of research has focused on social comparisons of emotions. Experiments have found that individuals affiliate under stressful conditions not simply to gain information about the situation they are in, but to define their emotional states (Schachter 1959; Zimbardo and Formica 1963). There is related evidence that affiliation is prompted by the need to reduce anxiety as well as compare emotions (Sarnoff and Zimbardo 1961; Teichman 1973; Zimbardo and Formica 1963), and that it does in fact reduce stress (Schachter 1959). Such research is relevant for managers because stress seems to be an occupational hazard of managerial work. Reorganizations, changes in leadership, and rumors of cutbacks in an organization can generate high levels of interaction, as anyone who has worked in an organization during such times can readily testify. Again, these interactions are prompted mainly by psychological, rather than informational, needs.

Another reason individuals interact is simply for entertainment. Human beings are social creatures, and many managers find talking pleasurable; more pleasurable, at least some of the time, than working alone. Gossiping, for some, is a very pleasant pastime. And while talking may contribute to the system's maintenance by communicating values and social rules in the organization, it is hard to understand in terms of expected material payoffs (March and Sevon 1984). However, there is some evidence that natural talkers are, in fact, rewarded in management careers. A twenty-ear follow-up study of Stanford M.B.A.s shows that those students who had scored highest on measures of sociability were most likely to become successful (i.e., highly paid) managers. In fact, this personality measure was a better predictor of success (within this highly selective sample) than scholastic aptitude. Success in business and probably in management careers in general, the authors of the study conclude, is more dependent upon relating effectively with people than solving scholastic puzzles with numbers or words (Harrell and Harrell 1984,30). One reason for the success of sociable managers may be that managers with strong social skills, because they are connected to a broader and deeper social network, are better at finding problems and defining them than managers with weak social skills. Solving problems, of course, is important for success, but skillful problem solving alone is not enough. The problems being solved have to be the right ones. Very smart but socially inept managers can easily set their sights on the wrong targets.

There are clearly many different motivations that prompt managerial interactions. Some interactions benefit the organization, the subunit, and/or the individual in some material way; some are a coping strategy in an ambiguous world; and others simply provide pleasure. But regardless of the motivation, interacting is clearly the mode of managerial work. As Mintzberg (1973) noted: "Unlike other workers, the manager does not leave the telephone or the meeting to get back to work. Rather, these contacts are his work" (p. 44).

NOTES

1. For example, see Carlson (1951), Cohen and March (1974), Stewart (1967), Mintzberg (1973), Horne and Lupton (1965), and Dubin and Spray (1964).

2. See Pounds (1969) and Webb and Weick (1979) for a discussion of the effect of deadlines on task priorities.

3. The continued success of the firms Peters and Waterman analyzed has been questioned in a *Business Week* article (November 5, 1984).

4. Because managers face different local environments, the system as a whole, through its subunits, typically reacts to multiple and diverse pressures simultaneously. This has two effects. It has a positive effect on the overall adaptability of the system, but it also makes systemwide coordination and control difficult.

5. Of course, there is no way of ascertaining whether their subjective assessments of what was important corresponded to what was important in an objective sense (actions that have significant consequences for the attainment of objectives). The virtual impossibility of making these objective assessments is one of the themes of this book.

6. The number of "more important" tasks initiated by others was greater than the number of "more important" tasks that managers initiated on their own, but the *flow* of important tasks from others and the *flow* of important self-initiated tasks were the same. (See chapter 7 for more discussion on the importance ratings of managers.)

7. See Fiske and Taylor (1984) for a review. The more extreme the behavior in either a positive or negative direction, the more salient it is (Fiske 1980). Some argue that negative stimuli are more salient than positive ones (Parducci 1968).

8. The reasoning here is similar to that used by economists in discussing public goods. That is, while private gains can result from complaints, the

gains, if any, that result from praise, that is, maintenance of good overall management practices, are mainly social. Just as we might expect an undersupply of public goods if only private means were relied upon, we would also expect generally low levels of praise in organizations.

9. This suggests the managers whose careers are in trouble would choose riskier actions than managers who have solid careers.

10. This does not mean that all individuals face the same consequences from a failure. Some individuals, say upper-level managers, who are regarded as having performed well in the past, may be able to bear more risk than individuals who have not yet established reputations as good performers. That is, a mistake would count more for an individual about whom there was little other performance information than an individual who had a track record of good performance. (This tendency is discussed in chapter 6.)

11. The explanations that are formed by managers who try to "learn" in a dynamic environment, however, are likely to be overly influenced by interpretations of what has happened in the past. People learn from feedback, but the lessons drawn are inferred through their beliefs and perceptions and these are largely the product of past experiences.

12. Economists, who have discussed incentives that affect information gathering, have emphasized the importance of the problem of getting the returns to the information collected. To do so, one needs to have a monopoly, or partial monopoly, over the information.

5

Supply Creates Demands

The preceding chapter focused on the reactive and interactive nature of managerial work and suggested reasons why administrative environments encourage these kinds of behavior. This chapter* takes a closer look at the interactive behavior of managers and elaborates on why it takes the form it does. It also illustrates how the interactive behavior of managers leads to administrative expansion.

Characteristics of Managerial Interactions

Managerial interactions have three fairly common characteristics. First, these interactions are generally oral, not written; second, most of them are generated by other managers within the same administrative system; and third, they often involve more than one other person. When coupled with the view, mentioned in chapter 4, that there is no natural limit to information acquisition and interpretation in an ambiguous world, the interactive behavior of managers has clear implications for the organizations in terms of pressures for growth.

Oral Versus Written Exchanges

Managers have a strong preference for oral communication; they rarely communicate with each other in writing. Perhaps this should not be surprising; oral communication has a number of distinct advantages over written communication. For one thing, it is faster. If managers are rewarded on the basis of their stock of information,

*I have drawn heavily on Hannaway (1987).

particularly new information, as I argued in chapter 4, it is to a manager's advantage to transmit the information while it is still "hot." In many cases, if a manager took the time to write the information down, especially in a formal report or in a memo, it would probably be known by relevant individuals in the organization long before the report or memo was disseminated. Transmitting commonly known information could have negative value both for the transmitter and the receiver. The receiver wastes time reading something she or he already knows and the transmitter appears "behind the times."

Another advantage of oral communication is that managers can be sure that their messages are received. There is no assurance that what they communicate in writing will ever be read. In fact, it probably will not be read; or, if it is read, it will probably not receive serious attention. Managers spend a relatively small fraction of their time reading, and when they do it, they typically do not consider it very important. (See chapter 7.) The managers I studied spent less than 2 percent[1] of their time reading material sent to them by other managers. Something in writing is more likely to be "for the record" or "for the files" than for the information it carries to other individuals. Items with information value are more likely to be communicated in person. One manager told me that, though he did not read most memos that came to him, he felt completely on top of what was going on in the organization. He was certain that if something important that he did not already know were in a memo, someone would be sure to call him to talk about it anyway.

A third advantage is that the spoken word carries less risk for a manager than the written word. Managers can think aloud, speculate, and "float" ideas without much fear of being held to whatever they have said; there is no unambiguous record. Managers can thus use oral exchanges more strategically than written ones. If they are questioned about oral statements they made at some previous time, they can always claim that they were misunderstood, or that the statements were out of context, and then reinterpret what they said in light of new information or new circumstances, perhaps couching the message in terms more persuasive to the recipient. Most politicians are quite skilled at this. Something in writing is different: there is evidence and, consequently, accountability. Even if managers change their positions on an issue as a result of new information or more experience, they may still have to explain their past views. Most experienced managers are understandably reluctant to put anything in writing unless they are very sure of it. Carrying on one's business orally can avoid many headaches in the future.

There are other advantages to oral exchange among managers. For one, it is easier. It usually requires less effort to ask a colleague about a particular rule or guideline or situation than it is to look it up in a manual or to try to figure it out on one's own. Another advantage is that oral channels carry a wider range of information than written channels. So by asking a colleague for help, one can find out not only what the rule is, but probably also how it is usually interpreted, how others have handled similar situations — maybe even how to get around a procedure. This inside information is seldom put into writing. How something is "really done" often differs, if only in subtle ways, from official procedures, but the difference can often make a manager's job much easier.

Internal Communications

Over 68 percent of the time that managers in this study spent in oral interaction they were participating in activities directed by managers from within the system; of these activities, 43 percent were self-initiated and 57 percent were initiated by other managers. (See Figure 5.1.) The internal nature of administrative work should probably not be surprising. Managers in the same system are more readily available for interaction than managers in other firms or workers in the production part of the organization. In-house managers also perform a number of functions that outside managers cannot. They provide inside information, collaborate in defining and solving problems, and share risk and responsibility. They are also messengers for each other. They can carry information about each other's successes, pet projects, and pet peeves to other parts of the organization and possibly influence organizational actions or each other's position in the organization in beneficial ways.

Large Group Interactions

Managers also tend to interact in large group meetings. A full third of the interaction time of managers in this study was spent in groups of at least five individuals. (See Figure 5.2.) Such gatherings

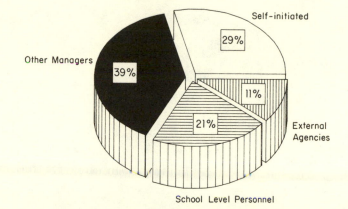

FIG. 5.1. Source of interaction activities. This is based on 85 percent of the data, in which I am able to identify the precise source. The response set to the initiator question was tailored to each manager so that "other" refers to different actors for different managers (see chapter 3). For example, it could refer to an in-house upper-level manager who was not on a particular manager's list or to someone outside. Because "other" was not exclusive of the other initiator categories, including it in this calculation could be misleading and it was therefore omitted.

were fairly common occurrences, accounting for over 20 percent of total managerial time in the system. Every Monday morning, for example, the superintendent met for at least two hours reviewing various matters with his cabinet, which was composed of the highest-ranking managers. Studies of managers in private industry show that they, too, spend a considerable amount of time in large group meetings. Rosemary Stewart (1967) found that her middle managers spent one-third of their time in group discussions with at least three people. And Mintzberg (1973) found that his chief executives spent 59 percent of their time in scheduled meetings that involved large groups.

Large meetings may appear to take up an unusually large portion of management resources, but they do have advantages. In fact, they might be a very efficient use of managers' time. Messages can be conveyed to all relevant parties at the same time, necessary coordination can be worked out on the spot, conflict and differing

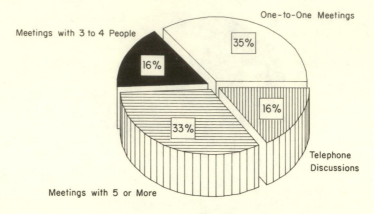

F<small>IG</small>. 5.2. Type of interaction activities.

opinions among affected groups can be voiced and incorporated, and managers can generally be kept informed about what is going on in various parts of the system. In addition, these gatherings can encourage the development of shared meanings, beliefs, and commitment to the organization.

Large group meetings may also further the private interests of individual managers, primarily by providing them with a large audience to which they can demonstrate their wares and wits. In fact, there may be an implicit understanding among managers that one of the main functions of meetings is to provide occasions for matching minds and dueling with words. With carefully chosen arguments and delivery styles, they can create favorable impressions of themselves and convince others how intelligent, creative, and/or reasonable they are. Meetings are the most public forums in which they can convey information about their abilities. One might expect, therefore, that the smarter managers would be more likely to convene and to attend large meetings. But this is not necessarily so. Even for those who are not as smart, there are advantages to attending meetings. Attendance itself may confer a certain degree of status, and nonattendance may carry a certain stigma (for reasons described later in this section). In addition, even if one does not engage in the forensic aspects of the meeting, one might acquire new information that could be used in other meetings. And being well-informed, if only for the purpose of not appearing to be "out of it," has its own value.

In addition to providing an arena in which to demonstrate individual worth or to collect information for use elsewhere, meetings also provide managers with opportunities to manipulate impressions of what has happened in the past and to generate support for particular positions they hold. As was mentioned in chapter 4, because explanations for the past are seldom clear cut, there is always room for interpretation. Similarly, there is always some uncertainty about the value of a particular position on an issue. Clever managers can selectively recall for the group incidents or events that put them or their preferred alternative in a favorable light and suppress unfavorable items (O'Reilly 1983). Managers no doubt do this unconsciously to some extent all the time, since individuals, in general, tend to recall information that supports their position more easily than they recall information that questions it (Bear and Hodun 1975). The impact of a persuasive manager in a large meeting can be quite significant. He or she might single-handedly be able to persuade the entire organization to adopt a particular interpretation of events. (Look at the influence that Ronald Reagan has had because of his communication skills.) The public nature of a large meeting confers some degree of legitimacy on whatever transpires there. Having a view expressed but not challenged at a meeting is often interpreted to indicate consensus. In addition, a view established at a meeting tends to be reinforced if a large number of individuals receive the same message and talk about it later among themselves. There is also a defensive side to attending meetings. A manager might attend a meeting to prevent another manager from wielding too much influence on a particular issue. In fact, his presence alone might guarantee that his interests will be looked after.[2]

Attendance at meetings also has symbolic importance. It indicates both to the managers themselves and to others that they are people whose views are important and that they are part of the "team," a quality highly valued in most management circles. Thus, managers are invited and attend meetings voluntarily even if they have nothing particular to say and no expectation of acquiring new information. Indeed, not inviting managers who think they have "participation rights" (Cohen, March, and Olsen 1972) may be more costly to the organization than inviting them. If they are not invited, they might take offense, feel excluded, and lower their level of effort! There might also be high costs to an individual manager for not attending meetings; it might suggest that he is *not* a "team player." "Good" managers dutifully attend the right meetings. A well-known General Motors executive who skipped meetings where he thought he had nothing to contribute suffered the consequences: "It quickly evolved that I wasn't a 'member of the team.' Management interpreted my absence from meetings as defiance. And there was a growing feeling that I wasn't interested in the work or contributing to the job . . . which impaired my ability to perform" (De Lorean 1979,29).

One certain consequence of large meetings, whether or not they are efficient for the organization or productive for the individual, is that they are very time-consuming: they can keep a large number of managers occupied in seemingly worthwhile activities for a large fraction of their time. It would be easy, for example, to add a number of additional managers to an administrative system and keep them "working" all day simply by inviting them to meetings where problems and issues were being interpreted and discussed. There is always uncertainty and always something that could be discussed further. The number of managers that could be added is probably only limited by the seating capacity of the conference rooms.

If managers were simply added to the system and consumed by it, they would be fairly costless (except for their salaries). But if a new manager behaved like the average manager on the job, that is, if the new manager interacted and reacted to the same extent as current managers, the new manager would create demands or costs for other managers simply because managers provide the bulk of the input for the work of other managers. Below I have used the data I collected to perform some very simple calculations that illustrate how, with few assumptions, the day-to-day work behavior of managers generates pressure for the expansion of administrative systems. Keep in mind that these figures are not presented to provide a precise quantitative estimate, but rather to illustrate a general process.

A Process of Administrative Expansion

Managers in this study spent, on average, 15 percent of their time initiating interactions; one-third were one-to-one meetings; one-third had five or more participants; and one-third was equally divided between telephone discussions and meetings with three or four people. Table 5.1 shows how this translates into demands on others in a forty-hour work week.

We can see that for every six hours of interaction time that a manager initiated in the system, more than three times that was created in terms of demands on others. It suggests the possibility that each additional manager could create more demands on the system than he contributes. Two scenarios—a best case and a worst case—illustrate this. Translating the proportion of time managers spent into hours, Table 5.2 shows the various ways that managers, on average, spent their time in a work week.

Best Case

If there were perfect substitution among managers, then we could assume that the 24.8 hours that the new manager spends reacting to requests from others would relieve some other manager of doing the same, and that the 9.2 hours spent on self-initiated non-interactive tasks would also relieve someone else in the system of the work performed during this time. Other managers in the system, therefore, would be relieved of 34 hours of administrative work as a

TABLE 5.1 Weekly Distribution of Manager-Initiated Interaction Activities

Type of Interaction	Hours/Week for Initiator	Hours/Week for Recipient
1-to-1 meeting	2.0	2.0
Meetings with 3 to 4	1.0	3.5
Meetings with 5 or more	2.0	12.0
Telephone	1.0	1.0
Total	6.0	18.5

TABLE 5.2   Average Hours/Week of Manager Initiation by Interaction

	Self	Other
Alone	9.2	8.4
Interacting	6.0	16.4
Total	15.2 hours/week	24.8 hours/week

result of hiring the new manager; this would be the new manager's gross contribution. If there were no second-round effects to the interactions that the new manager initiates, he or she would impose only 18.5 hours of new work on the system. (See Table 5.1.) Thus, in the best-case scenario, hiring a new manager for 40 hours would reduce the work pressure in the system by 15.5 hours.[3]

Worst Case

In the worst case, we could assume that the 16.4 hours in interactions that others initiate would be spent informing the new manager about the system or passing information on to him or her that is already known by someone else in the system. Giving the new manager the benefit of the doubt, we could assume that the time spent alone — both the 8.4 hours spent reacting, but not interacting, and the 9.2 hours spent on self-initiated solitary work — would be substituted for work that would have been done by some other manager. Under these assumptions, the new manager's gross contribution would be 17.6 hours. As in the previous case, he or she would consume 18.5 hours of other managers' time directly, but, in addition, we might assume that there would be second-round effects to this interaction. That is, the direct interactions of the manager would kick off another set of interactions; for example, the managers who received information from the new manager would pass that information on to others or try to verify it with others' opinions. On the first round the ratio of the initiator's interaction time to the recipient's interaction time would be 1 : 3 (Table 5.1). We might assume, somewhat generously, that the second-round ratio would be less, say 1 : 2, because some managers might know that the information was not "hot." This means that in addition to generating 18.5 hours (Table 5.1) of demands through direct inter-action with other managers, the manager would create 37 hours of demands indirectly. Only the 17.6 hours spent alone would be con-sidered a contribution to the system. Thus, in the worst case, hiring a new manager would result in a net increase of 37.9 hours of demands on the system.[4]

It is easy to imagine a situation in which an administrative system would be out of balance, perpetually facing excessive demands. In such a world, it would be no wonder if managers always felt hassled and pressured. The expected reaction to such a situation would be either to do more things in a superficial way or to find a way to relieve some of the demands in order to focus on fewer things. Most people would assume that the common sense way to do the latter would be to hire additional managers to absorb some of the work. But as we have seen, hiring additional managers into an administra-tive system may actually increase, rather than decrease, the de-mands in the system: in the best case, an additional manager work-ing a 40-hour week would only reduce demands in the system by 15.5 hours; in the worst case, the demands would increase by 37.9 hours. This is due, in large part, to the multiplier effects that seem to be an integral part of administrative work. Meetings typically involve more than one other person, and the work process is gener-ally more iterative than linear; that is, the work involves continuous searching for understanding more than producing some defined output. There is a natural asymmetry: it is easy for one manager to generate a considerable amount of work (although in a nonlinear system it is hard to say how much); yet it is difficult for any one manager to absorb much.

This tendency may be the basis for the growth of administrative systems; C. Northcote Parkinson seems to have thought so. But his best known remark — "Work expands so as to fill the time available for its completion" — does not fully explain his view of how admin-istrative systems function. The following is his description, in part facetious, of how an administrative office worked after seven subor-dinates were hired by Manager A:

> . . . for these seven make so much work for each other that all are fully occupied and A is actually working harder than ever. An incom-ing document may well come before each of them in turn. Official E

decides that it falls within the province of F, who places a draft reply before C, who amends it drastically before consulting D, who asks G to deal with it. But G goes on leave at this point, handing the file over to H, who drafts a minute that is signed by D and returned to C, who revises his draft accordingly and lays the new version before A. . . . What does A do? He would have every excuse for signing the thing unread, for he has many other matters on his mind. . . . But A is a conscientious man. Beset as he is with problems created by his colleagues for themselves and for him — created by the mere fact of these officials' existence — he is not the man to shirk his duty. He reads through the draft with care . . . and finally produces the same reply he would have written if officials C to H had never been born. Far more people have taken far longer to produce the same result. No one has been idle. All have done their best. And it is late in the evening before A finally quits his office and begins the return to Ealing. The last of the office lights are being turned off in the gathering dusk that marks the end to another day's administrative toil. Among the last to leave, A reflects with bowed shoulders and a wry smile that late hours, like gray hairs, are among the penalties of success. (Parkinson 1957, 5-7)

A picture similar to Parkinson's emerges from my data, with two major differences that are compatible with the ideas and observations of how administrative systems actually work: (1) the managers I observed seemed to be less concerned with written documents than with discussion; and (2) no linear process by which something tangible, such as a report, could be produced evinced itself in my study. The process of administrative work suggested by my data is more iterative than that suggested by Parkinson. It involves groping and probing. If the most important and most time-consuming part of a manager's job is developing an understanding of issues and defining problems, then the technology of managerial work must be far less clear than that implied by Parkinson's observation. A basic similarity in both of our observations is the interdependence of managerial work processes; the product, whatever it is, is jointly produced. Identifying the separate effects of individuals, however, is exceedingly difficult, especially when the work mode is predominantly oral and the objective is primarily understanding. So although the managers I studied and those in Parkinson's depiction were working hard and seriously, one has to suspect that at some point in administrative systems the marginal contribution of additional managers is negative. In a nonlinear system without clear measures of output, however, it is never known when this point is reached, nor is it obvious to the beleaguered manager.

Other Explanations for Administrative Expansion

The explanation for administrative growth suggested by my analysis is different from the explanation prevailing in the literature, which views the bureaucrat as a utility maximizer, interested in maximizing the size of the budget because as the budget increases so too does the power, salary, and perquisites of the bureaucrat's office (Tullock 1965; Downs 1967; Niskanen 1971, 1975; Williamson 1975). In short, there are incentives for expansion. This reasoning has most commonly been used to explain the growth of public bureaucracies; but it applies equally well to the private sector. Both public and private sector managers have scope for discretion enabling them to pursue their personal interests (within certain constraints). (See, e.g., Migue and Belanger 1974.) In the private sector, this scope is enhanced by market imperfections (Williamson 1964; Marris 1966); that is, if competition were perfect, managers would be able to pursue their private interests only insofar as they coincided with the firm's interests, because any firm that deviated from efficiency would not survive. This view associates organizational slack with imperfect competition (Selten 1985). In the public sector, a manager is provided with scope for discretion by the bureaucracy's bilateral monopoly relationship with its sponsor, for example, a legislature (Niskanen 1971).

The basic problem identified by economists is an old one; a conflict between the interests of individual managers and the interests of the organization. In the economics literature, these issues are often discussed in terms of problems of moral hazard or agency. Because of informational advantages, or as an economist would say, information asymmetries, managerial interests prevail; or, more accurately, these information asymmetries limit the control of the "principals" (i.e., shareholders, legislators whose interests coincide with the organization) over the managers. Managers simply know more about the operation of the organization, and others must rely on their judgment about how the firm should be run and how resources should be allocated. The implication is that the organization is less efficient than it might otherwise be; in particular, it may be operating with slack.[5]

Managers might also overinvest in administration for sociological reasons. These are reasons not typically used by economists, but certainly they fall within a broad definition of self-interest. For example, managers might simply enjoy working with individuals with whom they have more things in common—that is, other managers. Or, they might prefer more managers because interacting with and supervising individuals of higher status confirm their own sense of importance. The number of managers on the staff might indicate an individual manager's relative standing in the organization. The number of people managers supervise often indicates how much responsibility they have.

There is considerable evidence that could be construed as supporting the economist's explanation for bureaucratic growth. Indeed, a manager's salary, prestige, and power are, on average, a function of the size of the organization he or she heads.[6] This, however, is simply a correlation; it does not necessarily follow that increased organizational size will lead to a higher salary, etc. (I have seen no evidence relating specifically to administrative size.) Moreover, this kind of reduced-form analysis is, at best, of limited value when we come to the central question of analyzing the consequences of changes in organizational structure or design. No doubt the economic explanation is appealing partly because it is simple, and partly because it maligns the bureaucrat, a popular and socially acceptable scapegoat. On logical grounds, however, this thinking can be criticized. Simply asserting that some function is served by a particular practice is not the same as demonstrating that it is motivating the practice. While more power, for instance, may accrue to a manager as a result of an increase in the size of a bureau, power may not have been the reason the manager argued for a larger budget or more staff in the first place.

The view of much managerial behavior presented in this book is simpler. The managers appear as more benign, less calculating, individuals who are simply coping as best they can with the immediate demands of nearly boundless jobs while still limiting their personal liability for any adverse outcomes. They carry on without either a very good understanding of the relationship between the means and ends involved in the work or very clear feedback on the effects of most of their actions. They are almost always pressed and almost always uncertain. Managers typically respond to pressure by putting demands on others, sharing the work and the risks, and hiring help . . . and the situation becomes exacerbated. Bureaucratic expansion thus occurs as a by-product of managers' efforts to cope in an administrative environment of uncertainty and ambiguity and to attend to what most would agree are their job responsibilities. This does not mean that the power, prestige, and perquisites associated with greater size do not play a role in motivating and maintaining increased size, but rather that the same result can occur with more well-intentioned bureaucrats. It means there is pressure for administrative expansion even in the absence of a preference on the part of bureaucrats for it. Socially dysfunctional behavior can result from the combined actions of well-intentioned individuals simply coping with ambiguity and uncertainty.

Controlling Administrative Growth

Administrative expansion resulting from ongoing organizational processes is exceedingly difficult to control. The usual course of events is that managerial ranks grow steadily until there is a crisis, such as a series of sharp downturns in the firm's competitive position or a significant cutback in external funding. Then there are big cost-cutting moves that include reducing management positions.

One reason control is difficult is that managerial behaviors emanating from self-interest and from the organization's interests are in practice difficult to distinguish; that is, both lead managers to behave reactively and engage in interaction. Any attempt to control administrative expansion by putting a check on only the self-interested aspects of behavior, such as managers' marketing themselves or spreading risks, would be difficult at best. At worst, controls may interfere with the information sharing and joint problem solving that contribute to good decision making in the organization. Not only is it exceedingly difficult to distinguish self-interested behavior by observation; it is also probably nearly impossible to determine on a priori grounds what an organization's optimal rules might be for searching out information. In an ambiguously changing world, there is always something more to be known, and always some chance that an additional bit of information will lead to significantly better actions. But because the costs and benefits of additional information are not clear, the appropriate limits to searching are not easily knowable.

Viewing organizational behavior in terms of ongoing processes however, does suggest some courses of action. One is to direct managerial attention away from immediate concerns, which foster a myopic management view, and encourage aggregate measures based on an estimate of the combined effects of individual managerial behavior. This might be done, for example, by performing internal accountings, like that presented in this chapter, of the net resources used and released by hiring additional administrators. Some organizations have been known to set up meters in conference rooms that calculate and display the cost of the meeting (based on the salaries of participants) on a minute-by-minute basis (McKenzie 1972). Another strategy implied by the organizational process view is to decrease the risk-reducing aspects of managerial behavior by limiting criticism or punishment for managerial mistakes and/or to offer more praise for initiative and for tasks well done.

Variations in Expansive Tendencies

There are a number of factors implied in this and the preceding chapter that affect the expansive tendency and growth pattern of an administrative system. The functional responsibility of the managerial staff is one. The clearer the measures of output, the less prone the system would be to expansion. Managers in positions where performance measures are clearer, for example sales managers, probably behave differently from managers in positions where the separate contributions of individuals are less clear. With performance measures readily available, there would be less need for them to interact to broadcast their competence. They might also spend less time in meetings because the opportunity costs of their time are higher or, at least, better known. The clearer the performance measures, the more likely it is that managers will be rewarded on the basis of them and not on the basis of impressions or other indications only indirectly related to performance. The structure of an organization might also affect its expansive tendencies. If managers at different hierarchical levels face different levels of risk, as suggested in the next chapter, this would affect their behavior. Different levels of uncertainty facing the organization as a whole, such as

more highly dynamic external environments or more rapidly changing technologies, might also affect the disposition of the system to
expand by influencing the reactive and interactive tendencies of
managers. The limits to the growth process described here are probably the same as those described by other models of growth: budget
constraints and competition for resources (Niskanen 1971; Williamson 1975; Hannan and Freeman 1978).

Diffusion of Administrative Growth

While the data here are confined to growth within a single administrative system, it is not difficult to imagine the spread of this
growth among organizations, in a process similar to an armaments
race. Organizations, particularly public organizations, are in constant competition with other organizations for political and economic resources, so the race is often for information. Whichever
unit amasses more information has the advantage in negotiations
and in public relations. The unit with more information not only
can score more points, it can also throw the opposition off balance
with demands. As soon as one organization gains the advantage,
others in the negotiating game have to equip themselves to similar
levels to maintain their footing or even just to appear as though they
are in the same race. A race for information can also occur within
an organization as sets of coalitions compete with each other for
power and organizational resources.

We might expect the process of growth induced by competition
for information eventually to reach a state of equilibrium, but problems of indivisibility would probably retard it. That is, when an
additional management job is created, a full-time person is usually
hired, even though the demands the new manager was hired to
handle may not be full-time demands. This means the new manager
has excess capacity, and the excess can be used to generate additional demands . . . and so it goes. In an environment characterized by
organizations, especially public organizations, with ambiguous output, the diffusion or imitation of organizational forms is particularly likely to occur (DiMaggio and Powell 1983). In order to maintain or increase their legitimacy, these organizations will tend to
model themselves according to the administrative patterns of organizations viewed to be successful, even in the absence of evidence that
it will affect internal efficiency.

NOTES

1. This, in fact, might be an overestimate! Reading was in a response category that also included "thinking" and "planning." Together, from *all* sources, they accounted for 8.5 percent of managers' time on average.

2. If one is *very* influential in the organization, there might be less need to attend meetings. The views of the powerful are typically well known and those less powerful are hesitant to criticize them.

3. There is a "better" best case, which would be if the new manager attracted information into the system that was not currently there.

4. Although this is labeled the "worst case," there is still a "worse" worst case, in which the new manager does not substitute on an hour-to-hour basis with the old manager. An even worse case might be one in which managers were not substitutes in the sense that each would interpret information about problems or solutions differently and thereby kick off independent sets of search activities.

5. For examples of empirical research on this topic, see R. S. Ahlbrandt, "Efficiency in the Provision Fire Services," *Public Choice*, 19 (1973):1-42; and E. S. Savas, "Solid Waste Collection in Metropolitan Areas," in E. Ostrom (ed.), *The Delivery of Urban Services* (Beverly Hills, Calif.: Sage, 1976). For models in which managers get utility from slack (discretionary resources), see Niskanen (1975), Migue and Belanger (1974), and Weimer, David L. and C. Lawrence Evans, "Communication on Miller and Moe's 'Bureaucrats, Legislators, and the Size of Government'" (mimeographed, February 1985).

6. For example, see William H. Starbuck, "Organizational Growth and Development" in James G. March (ed.), *Handbook of Organizations* (Chicago: Rand McNally, 1965); and Robert Staaf, "The Public School System in Transition," in T. E. Bocherding (ed.), *Budgets and Bureaucrats: The Sources of Government Growth* (Durham, N.C.: Duke University Press, 1977).

6

Blinders and Biases

The last two chapters emphasized the highly interactive nature of work in administrative systems. Managers spend the great majority of their time exchanging information and generally surveying their environment. Yet, managers are often caught by surprise—in spite of their heavy investment in information exchange and surveillance. Surprises from the outside, such as changes in government regulations or new products from competitors, are understandable; organizations have limited control over their external environment. More difficult to understand are surprises from the inside, which is supposedly governed by the organization's controls. Yet stories of units within an organization working at cross-purposes, or of crises developing from minor problems that should have been identified, are commonplace. "Putting out fires" that should never have started is a significant part of a manager's job. This chapter* suggests some behavioral dynamics behind these "inside surprises."

Organizations, of course, attempt to prevent surprises. This is the main role that controls play within organizations; they direct behavior to ensure reliable performance. Two types of control are common: process control, which through operating procedures directs the way the work itself is carried out, and output control, which assesses what has been produced. Each of these control mechanisms works well under certain conditions. Process control can be used if the work is routine, as it is, for example, on an assembly line. Many other types of work can be similarly specified. Rental agreements and insurance forms, for example, direct the actions of car rental clerks, and under normal conditions, operating proce-

---

*I have drawn heavily on Hannaway (1985b).

dures determine the tasks even of airline pilots. These are all situations where the process of work is fairly well understood.

The second common way that organizations control participants' behavior is through their output. In some cases, the output can be determined by a design such as the specifications for the development of an engine. Contracts for goods and services also typically use this type of control. The assumption, of course, is that the output or the product is observable and can be evaluated in some real sense; that is, it is clear, after the fact, whether the job was properly done. Incentives based on task completion in organizations constitute another form of output control. Workers can be offered rewards commensurate with the quality or volume of their output. In these situations, the particular means that are used to produce the output need not be monitored. But, again, it is assumed that the output can be observed and measured. Salespersons, for example, are usually evaluated and compensated on the volume of their sales.

Neither process control nor output control is well suited to administrative systems. As argued earlier, actors in administrative systems typically operate without clear feedback about their product and without a clear technology or process to guide their behavior. Because of these conditions, and in addition because a good many of the problems they face are unpredictable, it is difficult to design control systems for administrative behavior. Scott (1981), drawing on research he conducted with Dornbusch in a number of different types of organizations (Dornbusch and Scott 1975), described settings where performance evaluations and therefore control systems were problematic because of excessive complexity and interdependence of tasks, lack of goal clarity, and high uncertainty. He explained that "the more difficult it is to determine whose performance has contributed to a particular outcome, or to determine what sort of outcome is desired, or to predict how a given desired outcome may be accomplished, the more difficult it is to design an adequate system of control . . . " (Scott 1981,286). These conditions are common in administrative systems. Nevertheless, administrative systems function; managers are typically very busy and they appear to have direction. What directs what they do?

Since uncertainty about the production process and ambiguity about outcomes restrict the development of formal controls such as rules and procedures, most directives that managers receive about what they should do on a day-to-day basis on the job tend to be informal. These typically take the form of negotiation and give and take among organizational participants. Managers manage each other; they are both the controllers and the controlled. They are engaging in a form of process control, but without a very clear understanding of the means of production. The main advantage of less formal means of coordinating and controlling activities is that they allow for flexibility, so that unanticipated situations can be accommodated. Their main disadvantage is that they are costly, requiring extensive person-to-person interaction. And the descriptions of managers at work presented here and elsewhere do, indeed, show that interaction activities consume most of their time.

The lack of objective organizational standards of performance is a two-edged sword for managers. It allows managers some freedom to pursue private interests, but it also creates considerable uncertainty for them. And under conditions of uncertainty, this chapter will show, social cues and the social structure play a large role in defining appropriate behavior (Kiesler and Kiesler 1969; Thompson and Tuden 1959; Festinger 1950, 1954; Pfeffer, Salancik, and Leblebici 1976).

The patterns of behavior that emerge in administrative systems are not necessarily those that would be expected of a tightly run, rational system. I uncovered three patterns in my data that can contribute in significant ways to the likelihood of inside surprises. First, upper-level managers[1] were only loosely connected with the other parts of the organization. They spent much of their time being controlled by and controlling other upper-level managers. Second, lower-level managers were hesitant to refer problems or to seek out others when they confronted unusual issues. In fact, lower-level managers who confronted the greatest levels of uncertainty in their work were the least likely to refer matters to others or to seek help. Third — and this may make matters worse — lower-level managers were also reluctant to tackle nonroutine matters on their own. This reluctance might on average be functional for the organization, but it probably also leaves many problem situations festering. Together, these findings suggest that managers at the top, who are responsible for forming strategy and coordinating activities at the organizational level, are doing so with only limited and perhaps biased information about what is going on in their organization, with the result that many problems are left completely unattended. With patterns such as these, the frequent occurrence of "inside" surprises is not at all surprising.

This chapter focuses on these three patterns. As in earlier chapters, I present my data and interpret them in light of other research findings, and then I discuss their implications for the system in general. Two factors are central to the discussion in this chapter. One is the manager's position in the organization, which can give us insight into traditional hierarchically based control; the other is the novel or nonroutine nature of the manager's tasks, which permits us to look at the system as a problem-solving entity.

The traditional depiction of an organization is a chart in the shape of a pyramid that represents the authority structure of the organization. Though fewer in number, those in upper-level positions are viewed as having the legitimate power — the right — to make things happen in the organization. They are also commonly viewed as having both the knowledge about what should happen and the incentives to make it happen. The presumption then is that those in higher offices direct and control the work behavior of those in lower-level positions. According to Weber, such a hierarchy of offices is a basic bureaucratic characteristic: "The principles of office hierarchy and of levels of graded authority mean a firmly ordered system of super- and subordination in which there is supervision of the lower offices by the higher ones" (Weber 1947,197). But how well does this describe the workings of an administrative system? Are there differences between the *demand structure*, that is, the extent to which different managers direct the attention of other managers, and the *hierarchical structure* of the organization? Do upper-level managers direct and control the work behavior of lower-level managers? And how is the behavior of upper-level managers directed?

An alternative to the traditional view is what I will call the problem-solving model. This model suggests that under certain conditions upper-level managers are more likely to receive tasks than initiate them. It implicitly assumes that the occurrence of problems cannot be predicted with much accuracy and that appropriate responses cannot always be specified in advance. Situations are handled as they come up and tasks are directed to those who can best handle them. Thus, the behavior of managers depends on the characteristics of the task at hand. In this view, nonroutine work bubbles up; it is referred to the top of the system for resolution, whereas more routine matters are handled sufficiently well at the lower levels. Given the relatively high levels of nonroutine work in administrative systems, upper-level managers are thus, on average, kept pretty busy handling task referrals and spend less time referring tasks to others.

Two themes that emerged earlier in the book are pertinent here, both relating to how the social structure of the system affects the information structure. One theme is risk sharing, in which managers interact to share the risks associated with actions they take; the other is "broadcasting," in which managers interact in order to display their competence. Risk sharing is particularly likely at upper levels where it leads to a lateral flow of work. In the case of the lower-level managers, however, broadcasting is more prevalent than risk sharing, and this leads to biases in the type of tasks and the type of information that flow upward in the system. Lower-level managers interact freely about matters that show their competencies; but they are reluctant to broadcast their inability to handle issues alone. This makes them hesitant to run to the boss for help in solving problems. While it would generally be to a manager's advantage to share any risks associated with unusual problems, the costs to a lower-level manager's reputation by displaying ignorance are too high. These ideas are discussed further later in this chapter.

Segregation of the Top

As discussed earlier, most of the work that managers in this study carried out was undertaken at the request or direction of someone else. Classical bureaucratic theory suggests that this would be the case for those in lower levels in the system, at least more strongly than it would be for those in upper levels. The data, however, show the opposite. Almost three-quarters (71.7 percent) of the work of upper-level managers was directed by others; for lower-level managers, it was less, 64.2 percent.[2] Table 6.1 identifies who these "others" are and shows the extent to which they made demands on upper-

TABLE 6.1   Percentage Distribution of "Other"-Directed Work by Source*

Source	Upper-Level Managers (N = 19)	Lower-Level Managers (N = 33)
Inside	**53.2**	**26.5**
Upper	37.3	12.9
Lower	14.3	13.2
Other insiders	1.4	.4
Board of Education	.2	-0-
Technical Core	**10.0**	**27.0**
School level	10.0	27.0
External Environment	**8.5**	**10.3**
Parents/students	1.4	1.9
Community/Advisory boards	.5	3.9
Federal/state resource	4.3	3.0
Special project	.3	1.0
Other outsiders	2.0	.5
Total	71.7	64.2

*This is based on the 85 percent of the data in which I can identify the precise source of "other"-directed work.

and lower-level managers. Upper-level managers were the primary directors (37.3 percent) of the attention and work behavior of other upper-level managers. They were the main providers of information, problems, solutions, and comfort for each other.[3] The effect on upper-level managers of lower-level managers (14.3 percent) and of individuals in the technical production part of the organization (10 percent) was considerably less.

Other behavioral studies of managers have reported similar tales suggesting that upper-level managers travel in packs. Cohen and March (1974), for example, found that college presidents spent 40 percent of their time with senior college administrators. Burns (1954) conducted a study of the top members of an executive group in an engineering factory and found that they spent between a quarter and two-fifths of their time interacting with each other (p. 86). In a subsequent study of the top management groups in eight firms, Burns again noted that they tended to be segregated from lower-level management (1957,60).

There are three possible explanations for the high level of interdependence among upper-level managers. The first is that considerable interaction and shared decision making is necessary at that level to coordinate the activities of the organization; it is quite reasonable to assume that the heads of different divisions need to work out among themselves the alignment and realignment of work processes. A second explanation is simply that upper-level managers enjoy being with each other. In a study of college presidents, Cohen and March (1974) argued that pleasures in the perquisites of the office had an important effect on the overall patterns of time allocation of these executives. Feeling free to call on upper-level managers is a perquisite that comes with being an upper-level manager; like getting a key to the executive washroom or using the executive dining room, it is a reflection of the manager's achievement, success, and importance, similar to what Fred Hirsch (1976) called a "positional good."[4] Upper-level managers are not the only highly ranked individuals who behave this way. Studies of communication patterns (Barnlund and Harland 1964; Allen and Cohen 1969) show that high-status individuals in general communicate more with each other than with low-status individuals, perhaps for the same reasons.[5] A third explanation, which was discussed at length earlier, is that there is safety in numbers. Managers protect themselves from downside risks by making decisions and engaging in tasks jointly; others are implicated and incur part of the risk. Retribution is weakened since it is highly unlikely that a significant part of the senior staff would be fired. Upper-level managers who want to share risks generally can only do so with managers of at least equal position. With the exception perhaps of a technical expert, a lower-ranked manager cannot assume responsibility for the actions or lack of action of a superior. Risk sharing by those in upper levels is thus largely constrained within that rank.

The segregation — largely voluntary — of upper-level management has a number of important implications for organizations. First, it clearly affects the extent and type of knowledge that upper-level managers have about the functioning of the organization. Upper-level managers are likely to be very knowledgeable about the concerns and interests of their colleagues, even those who represent different parts of the organization. This is certainly important for effective coordination and organization-wide strategic decision making. On the other hand, upper-level managers run the risk of developing a "group think" mentality whereby, perhaps unwittingly, they mutually reinforce a particular view of the world and systematically screen out alternative perspectives (Janis and Mann 1977). The strong belief among NASA officials in the invincibility of the space program prior to the Challenger accident was probably partly the result of such a process. In addition to the psychological effects of reinforcing certain views within the group, one also has to think about the actual value of information that upper-level managers share with each other. Much of it must be redundant. Upper-level managers are tied into the same sources—each other. One has to suspect that it would pay for them to exploit their weaker ties with managers at lower levels, where there would be less redundancy in the information they would receive (Granovetter 1973). Yet only exceptional upper-level managers do so. Popular accounts report that this, indeed, is one of the characteristics that distinguishes those managers who are most successful. They "manage by wandering around" (MBWA), presumably collecting information that is not carried by their usual channels (Peters and Waterman 1982; Peters and Austin 1985).

In general, the connection between upper-level managers is stronger than that between them and lower-level managers. The picture that emerges from the data is not a traditional simple hierarchical model. Lower-level managers worked at the direction of upper-level managers only a small part of the time (12.9 percent). In fact, the data show that lower-level managers had a greater effect on those in upper levels (14.3 percent) than the reverse. Upper-level managers may have had more formal power, that is, greater potential for influence because of their position; but lower-level managers exercised more direct influence by controlling a heavier flow of demands. This flow of tasks from bottom to top is what we might expect from what I have called the problem-solving model of behavior in an administrative system. Such a model assumes that different types of tasks are handled in different ways; some tasks, particularly nonroutine tasks, go up, and others go down. In the next two sections, we look at how routine and nonroutine tasks are processed in the system.

Inhibited Search and Flow at Lower Levels

According to a problem-solving model, when managers confront tasks that they are uncertain how to handle, they search for clarification and direction, most commonly by asking others. The nature of the task prompts problem-solving behavior. It would seem to follow that those managers who deal with uncertain tasks more often would also initiate interactions with others more often. But this expectation is confirmed only in the data describing the behavior of upper-level managers, not in the data on lower-level managers. And we are particularly concerned here with the behavior of lower-level managers. That is, the loose overall connection between upper- and lower-level managers would not be a problem if lower-level managers connected with those in upper levels, or at least conferred with colleagues at their own level, when dealing with the nonroutine aspects of their work, so as to get advice in situations where their experience did not provide guidance. But the lower-level managers I studied did not behave this way.

Figures 6.1 and 6.2 show the relationship between the level of uncertainty a manager perceived in a task and the extent of search behavior, that is, self-initiated interaction, that upper- and lower-level managers exhibited. The relationship between uncertainty and

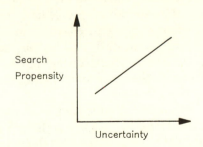

Fig. 6.1. Uncertainty and search: Upper-level managers. See Hannaway 1985 for the regression results on which these are based.

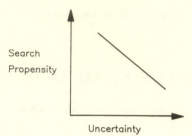

FIG. 6.2. Uncertainty and search: Lower-level managers. See Hannaway 1985 for the regression results on which these are based.

search is in the opposite direction for upper- and lower-level managers. Upper-level managers who dealt with higher levels of task uncertainty engaged in greater search; but lower-level managers who dealt with higher levels of task uncertainty were more reticent. Lower-level managers who dealt with greater levels of uncertainty were *less* likely to engage in search behavior than lower-level managers with less uncertainty.[6]

Why was this the case? Why did upper- and lower-level managers behave so differently under conditions of uncertainty? One answer is related to the importance of "broadcasting" for lower-level managers; at least some managers interact to market themselves, broadcast their competence, and promote their ideas. They are reluctant to interact about uncertain issues because it may display their ignorance. A recent *Fortune* magazine article claimed that as investment banking houses have grown and aged, there are more senior people sitting around the table, and junior people have become less confident and more hesitant to participate actively in discussions. They think, "I can't afford one mistake. It'll be the end of my career" (Sherman 1986). Lower-level managers are more likely to interact about matters in which they feel some confidence and can show what they know.

While my data do not identify those with whom lower-level managers initiated interaction when dealing with certain and uncertain tasks,[7] other researchers have noted the reluctance of lower-level managers to bring problematic issues to their bosses. (See Glauser 1984 for review.) Sayles (1964) argues that "managers believe they are evaluated on how few problems they cause" (p. 188). And studies of organizational communication have shown that the accuracy and substance of upward communications in an organization is affected by trust in one's superiors, the superior's influence over one's future, and one's mobility aspirations (O'Reilly and Roberts 1973). In general, information favorable to the sender is more likely to be sent upwards than information that is unfavorable. So, if lower-level managers feel that their unwillingness or inability to handle a nonroutine matter alone undermines their eligibility for a higher position, they will be reluctant to ask for help. In fact, Wilensky (1967) reported one study in which there was a direct correlation between holding back "problem" information and career mobility: "Men on their way up were prone to restrict information about such issues as lack of authority to meet responsibilities, fights with other units, unforeseen costs, rapid changes in production, scheduling or work flow, fruitless progress reports, constant interruptions, insufficient time or budget to train subordinates, insufficient equipment or supplies, and so on" (p. 43). The reluctance of lower-level managers to communicate upwards is perhaps reinforced by the chilly reception they often receive. A study of managerial attitudes toward communication episodes found that managers generally had the most positive attitude toward interactions they initiated themselves and the least positive to those initiated by subordinates (Lawler, Porter, and Tennenbaum 1968). If these attitudes are conveyed to subordinates, which is likely, it no doubt buttresses the reluctance of lower-level managers to communicate upward.

Upper-level managers, on the other hand, are not so inhibited. There are a couple of reasons why this might be the case. First, many of them have reached the peak of their careers and probably are not so concerned about promotion. And if, as March and March (1978) claim, promotions are almost random at upper levels in the hierarchy, their behavior is quite reasonable. Upper-level managers are in a position where they have more to lose than to gain. It is difficult for them to distinguish themselves by superior performance, but their power and credibility in the organization could be affected by mistakes. As a consequence, they worry more about being identifiably responsible for a mistake than about enhancing their promotion chances. In their case, risk sharing dominates broadcasting.[8] Second, the reception upper-level managers receive when they initiate an interaction is different from what lower-level managers receive. Managers rate interactions initiated by peers and superiors more highly than they do those initiated by subordinates (Lawler, Porter, and Tennenbaum 1968), which suggests that the interactions senior managers initiate are probably greeted cordially, and thus encourage further interaction. In addition, there is probably a quid pro quo relationship about interactions among upper-level managers: "I'll listen to your concerns and help you out and, in turn, you'll listen to mine." Certainly norms for being a "team player" are well recognized and cultivated in the upper levels of organizations. Thus, the consequences of initiating interactions may be different for upper- and lower-level managers. Upper-level managers may be praised for seeking advice and encouraging participation of others in decision making, whereas lower-level managers may be criticized for not working independently.

Routine and Nonroutine Work

Managers considered almost two-thirds (65.8 percent) of the work they performed to be routine. (See Figure 6.3.) As might be expected, from both a hierarchical model and a problem-solving model, there were differences between upper- and lower-level managers. Upper-level managers engaged in a greater proportion of nonroutine work (44 percent) than did lower-level managers (28 percent). A question we might ask here is where this nonroutine work comes from. Is it undertaken at the managers' initiative? Or is it referred to them from others? Figure 6.3 shows that nonroutine work is almost three times as likely to be referred to managers than it is to be initiated by them: 11 percent of the work of upper-level managers was nonroutine and self-directed, 32 percent of their work was nonroutine and initiated by someone else. The pattern for lower-level managers is similar. On first inspection, this makes managers appear conservative; that is, they tend to stick to routine work unless someone imposes nonroutine work on them.

If, however, we assume that the amount of time managers spend reacting is fixed in the sense that they feel compelled to respond at least on some level to the demands of others (because, as discussed

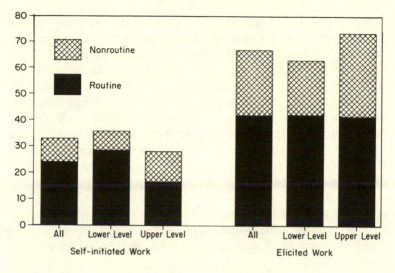

FIG. 6.3. Proportion of routine and nonroutine tasks in self-initiated and elicited work.

in chapter 4, once an issue is referred to them they feel liable for it), then we see something different. The rates of routine and nonroutine work *within* the initiated and elicited categories are shown in Table 6.2.[9] The rates at which upper-level managers initiated nonroutine tasks (42 percent) was about the same as the rate at which they responded to nonroutine tasks (44 percent). But the rate at which lower-level managers responded to nonroutine tasks (33 percent) was 50 percent higher than the rate at which they undertook

TABLE 6.2   Proportion of Routine/Nonroutine Task Initiated and Elicited

	Self-Initiated		Elicited	
	R	NR	R	NR
All managers	.73	.27	.62	.38
Lower-level	.79	.21	.67	.33
Upper-level	.58	.42	.56	.44

nonroutine work on their own (21 percent). This suggests that the type of work in which upper-level managers engage, whether it is routine or nonroutine, is not much affected by whether they are doing it at the behest of someone else or on their own initiative, but the type of work that lower-level managers undertake is significantly affected. Lower-level managers are only half as likely as upper-level managers to engage in a nonroutine task at their own initiative. (See Figure 6.4.) If lower-level managers are not directed to do otherwise, they have a strong tendency to stay with the routine aspects of their work. This implies that if lower-level managers follow the advice of many "how to" management consultants and devise ways to control more of their own activities, rather than letting themselves be directed by others, the amount of nonroutine work performed in the system will be reduced and probably along with it the amount of innovation and the adaptive capacity of the system.

One might argue that confining lower-level managers to routine work works quite well most of the time. Under normal circumstances, standard procedures should accommodate most lower-level management work. And generally speaking, it may not be a good idea to have lower-level personnel undertaking nonroutine work on their own. For one thing, it is very likely to affect the number and severity of problems associated with coordination and quality control, which might more than offset the benefits of greater initiative at lower levels. Few organizations want too many lower-level "lone

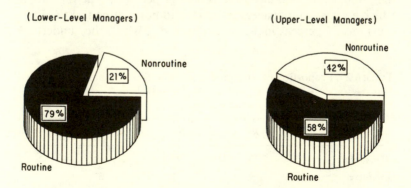

Fɪɢ. 6.4. Proportion of self-initiated routine and nonroutine work.

rangers" or "loose cannons" off tackling issues on their own. The Ollie Norths and John Poindexters of the world can cause serious problems for their superiors.

Under other conditions, however, there are serious problems associated with the reluctance of lower-level managers to take on nonroutine work. One such problem is referred to as the "peak load" problem in other areas: what works well for the normal flow of events is not sufficient for heavier flows; yet it is inefficient to be continually geared up for increased demands. This problem, of course, is relatively simple to solve when the heavier flows are predictable, for example, in traffic or computer use. But in the case of managerial work, the occurrence of more demanding tasks, that is, nonroutine situations requiring higher levels of effort, discretion, and sophistication, cannot always be predicted. Unpredictable, nonroutine matters are difficult for any system to handle, but they may be particularly difficult in administrative systems because the sensors that should provide warning signals do not work well. That is, if lower-level managers neither take on nonroutine situations on their own nor seek help from others, consequential issues that emerge at lower levels are suppressed. Only those that develop into crises come to the attention of upper-level management, and they often come without warning.

There has been little research on self-correcting mechanisms in organizations, with the noted exception of Albert Hirschman's important book *Exit, Voice, and Loyalty*. Hirschman identifies "exit," the withdrawal of consumers or members from the organization, and "voice," the overt expression of dissatisfaction, as alternative ways that management learns of the problems and failings of the organization. The book primarily discusses the conditions under which one option is more likely to occur than the other; Hirschman implicitly assumes one of these forms of correction will occur. A further option available to those who are dissatisfied, however, is silence (Kolarska and Aldrich 1980), which Hirschman does not consider, and there are conditions under which it is more likely than either exit or voice. This option is open to and likely to be taken often by actors in hierarchical systems, and it can seriously retard the recuperative capacity of the system.

Other researchers have noted lack of assertiveness in taking on nonroutine tasks as a basic problem in administrative hierarchies

(Sayles 1964; Warwick 1975). The explanation given by sociologists (Crozier 1964; Blau 1963; Merton 1968) is based on insecurity in social relations. Individuals who feel insecure because of their newness on the job or because of their minority status might exhibit the same lack of assertiveness as lower-level managers. Rules and routines protect individuals in socially inferior positions from arbitrary treatment by supervisors by marking the boundaries of their jobs (Crozier 1964,55). Such boundaries, either formally defined or defined by common practice, demark individuals' areas of responsibility; they cannot be held accountable for situations outside their normal scope of duties. Generally, then, lower-level managers are not at risk for not taking on nonroutine matters because such matters are not part of their jobs. Crozier and Sayles both found that lower-level managers resist blurring the lines of their job responsibilities; they have almost complete discretion within the rules of their area, and they guard this territory. Blurred or broken boundaries not only put them on unfamiliar ground, they also invited surveillance and personal supervision from above. These are things lower-level managers try to avoid.

Solutions

The central point of this chapter is that in the absence of controls well grounded in either the production process or the outputs of an administrative system, the social structure of the system plays an important role in determining work flow. But the social structure also introduces certain blinders and biases into the system that contribute to the likelihood of "surprises." In general, the blinders and biases stem from the weak connection between what goes on in the lower levels of an administration system and what goes on in the upper levels. In order to remedy this situation, corrective mechanisms are probably needed at both levels.

The U.S. State Department, for one, has set procedures in place to minimize the way bureaucracies stifle information and opinions at the bottom. For example, the Secretary's Open Forum encourages differences of opinion by publishing papers, sponsoring discussions, and inviting critics to speak. There is also a "dissent channel" through which one can send messages over the heads of one's superiors directly to the secretary and his or her top aides, supposedly without fear of being penalized. The American Foreign Service Association also gives four awards annually to Foreign Service officers "who buck the bureaucracy or display exceptional initiative" (Taubman 1981). While no doubt meritorious, these procedures are one-sided, encouraging those in lower levels to take action while the upper levels sit as passive recipients.

It is interesting to see how managers reputed in some circles to be successful have handled the problem. Harold Geneen, the former chief executive officer at ITT, reported that ITT had a basic policy of "no surprises." He claims that "ninety-nine percent of all surprises in business are negative" (1984,94). He implemented his "no surprise policy" through a system of "red flags." Each month managers from each and every division or profit center in the corporation were instructed to "red flag" their problems at the beginning of their reports. And woe be to the manager if a significant problem came to the attention of the top management that had not been "red flagged." What Geneen did was to change the risks associated with action and inaction. It became far riskier for a lower-level manager not to report problems than to be straightforward about them. In this way, problematic information was forced upwards. There is, of course, a delicate balance. If too many "red flags" are sent up, upper levels become overloaded and have difficulty sorting out the more serious problems.

Geneen also recognized that communication in organizations had to be a two-way street. Lower levels had to be encouraged to send problem information up, but upper levels also had to be encouraged to reach down. Geneen himself often went down to lower levels for face-to-face discussions so as not to rely only on interpretations of events by his top management people. "At ITT, we cut through two or three levels of upper management, so that my management team and I could talk and deal directly with the men on the firing line, the men who were responsible for the performance of their divisions and profit centers" (1984,91).

One of the reasons, perhaps, for the importance of corporate cultures in successful firms is that they foster more trusting communication patterns and, as a consequence, management is kept better informed about the strengths and weaknesses in the organization's operation. There is an assumption that when members identify with the organization the level of goal incongruency within the organization is low; they see themselves as part of the same team. This common understanding reduces self-interested behavior and promotes productive social relations, providing a form of control that Barnard (1962) recognized as to some extent essential to the operation of every organization (p. 148). Ouchi (1980) has gone further and argues that what he calls a clan form of control, one where participants through socialization come to share goals, may be the most efficient form of control when performance ambiguity is high.

NOTES

1. Upper- and lower-level managers are described in the Appendix.

2. These figures were based on responses where the respondents identified the source; that is, responses in the general "other" category were excluded from this analysis. When these responses are included, the total of "other directed" work combines to a slightly higher percentage of the total.

3. The actual amount of time upper-level managers spent together was actually greater because it also included some fraction of the self-initiated time.

4. For an extended and interesting discussion of the effect of status seeking on a wide range of human behavior, see Frank (1985).

5. The instrumental explanation for interaction behavior, that is, for task and program coordination, and the status-revelling explanation are here empirically indistinguishable.

6. This particular finding was based on analysis of fifty of the fifty-two managers. Two managers were excluded because of some identifiable idiosyncracies associated with their behavior that would be misleading for this particular analysis. For example, the superintendent credited himself as the initiator of regularly scheduled meetings so he would show particularly high levels of search behavior in this analysis. Because these meetings occurred weekly, regardless of the amount of uncertainty facing the superintendent, their relationship to the superintendent's sense of uncertainty for the particular weeks I studied would simply be spurious.

7. My data only reported the interaction as self-initiated.

8. This may be related to Tversky's experimental finding that individuals are averse to risk when seeking gains (Kahneman and Tversky 1984).

9. For example, the rate of routine initiation here simply is $a/(a+b)$, where for each manager a = the count of observations of routine initiations and b = the count of nonroutine initiations. And the nonroutine reaction is $d/(c+d)$, where for each manager c = the count of routine tasks that were elicited and d = the count of nonroutine tasks that were elicited.

7

The Importance of
Being Important

This chapter focuses on managerial assessments of importance:
What aspects of their work do managers consider more important
and what aspects do they consider less important? Ratings of importance indicate how involved managers are in the various tasks
they undertake. Previous studies of managerial behavior, by reporting only time allocations, have implicitly assumed that managers
give equal weight to all tasks and that the level of managerial effort
given to a task is demonstrated solely by the amount of time devoted to it (Sproull 1984). This, of course, can be very misleading.
Managers deal with some tasks in a very offhanded manner, whereas other tasks command their full attention. The importance measure shows these distinctions.[1]

The system, as described in the preceding chapter, was segmented; upper- and lower-level managers were only weakly connected to
each other. Upper-level managers kept mainly to themselves, directly controlling only a small proportion of the work conducted by
lower-level managers; and lower-level managers were reluctant to
interact and seek assistance when they were handling nonroutine
matters. This chapter also considers the linkages among managers,
but it is specifically concerned with the importance that managers
attach to the connections that are made. How, for example, do
upper-level managers rate the interactions they have with those on a
lower level? How do they rate the time they spend alone? Are some
content areas considered more important than others?

In this chapter I rely particularly heavily on the data I collected. I
refer to a few studies that have investigated factors that affect indi-

108

viduals' level of involvement in their tasks, but I found no studies that were explicitly concerned with managerial ratings of the importance of their tasks and their related behavior. Each time managers responded to a random signal and recorded what they were doing, they rated its importance, as explained in chapter 3. Managers assessed the task at hand relative to their "model" task. They were told to ask themselves, "Is this more or less important than what I usually do?" Managers therefore made a subjective assessment of the importance of each task and judged it relative to the other tasks involved in their jobs. They were not asked to judge it relative to tasks that other managers in the organization perform.

Distribution of Important Work

Managers rated about a quarter of their work (25.75 percent), on average, "more important" than what they "usually" do, and they considered 9.41 percent "less important." Upper-level managers considered a higher proportion "more important" (31.1 percent) than did lower-level managers (22.2 percent), and they also considered a higher proportion "less important" (11.02 percent) than did lower-level managers (8.05 percent).[2] (See Figure 7.1.) The rest of the chapter discusses the factors according to which managers determine a task's importance, but the distribution of work considered to be more and less important is interesting in its own right. It shows that managers do, indeed, discriminate among their tasks and that a sizable minority of their tasks are likely to receive special attention. This is the case for both upper- and lower-level managers.

Managers might consider a task important (i.e., be more involved in it) for a number of reasons. Some of these reasons are probably similar to the reasons social psychologists give for why individuals pay particularly close attention to some stimuli, such as certain types of advertisements and not others. (See Fiske and Taylor 1984 for review.) Ego involvement, for example, has been shown to affect peoples' assessments of importance (Sherif and Hovland 1961), so managers would tend to be particularly involved in tasks related to projects that they developed. Involvement would also be greater if the issue at hand were central to the manager's beliefs (Kiesler,

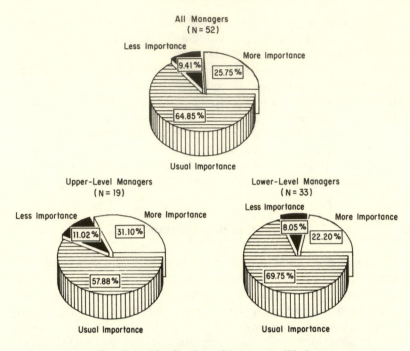

FIG. 7.1. Distribution of Important Work.

Collins, and Miller 1969); for example, an issue concerned with minority achievement or the worth of a particular planning model may be dear to the hearts of some managers. A third factor that also affects importance ratings is the consequences of a task either for the individual or for the organization (Zimbardo 1960); the award of a contract from an external agency, for example, may have significant individual and/or organizational consequences.

In this study I did not take measures that would indicate the psychological processes mentioned above, such as measures of ego involvement and beliefs. Rather, I used a structural approach. My underlying assumption was that the psychological effects of specific types of tasks are similar for all individuals, or, at least, the effect of task characteristics is strong enough to show a pattern of managerial response in spite of any individual differences among managers.

Thus, I report the distribution of levels of involvement (importance) according to types of *tasks*, not according to *individuals* with different psychological makeups. What types of issues and activities grab managers? What are the characteristics of those that do not?

Determinants of Importance

Managers receive tasks from a variety of channels, and in a variety of forms and content areas. Do these factors affect managers' judgments of importance in systematic ways? This section addresses this question by describing the ways in which managers determine the importance of their tasks, that is, by source (e.g., superiors); by activity (e.g., large meetings); and by content (e.g., budget concerns).[3]

By Source

The relationship between the source of a task and its importance rating is of particular interest. As argued in chapter 6, the social structure of the system plays a large role in directing managerial behavior. This is because there is uncertainty about appropriate managerial actions and their value, so traditional controls (i.e., either monitoring the process or evaluating output) are plagued with difficulties. The findings here suggest that social structure also affects importance ratings. The rank of the individual carrying out the task is associated with how others judge the task's importance. This is not surprising. The importance of different people in an organization is fairly easy to infer through rank, while the importance of a particular issue or the expected value of a particular way of handling it is typically far less clear. People—perhaps more than the issues themselves—direct the intensity with which managers engage in the various aspects of their work.

The effect of social structure is especially evident when new employees enter an administrative system. One of the first things newcomers typically pick up is *who* is important and to *whom* they should pay particular attention. If an individual's output were more easily observable, the orientation of new employees might be different. In particular, more attention might be given in these settings to the technical aspects of work and/or the production expectations and less attention to who the actors are. I know of no available evidence on this, but a study of the socialization, especially informal socialization, of new employees in settings with different task and output characteristics might provide some interesting results. How much of on-the-job socialization is concerned with the "whos" and how much with the "whats"?

Figures 7.2a and b show the average level of importance that managers in my study attached to tasks received from different sources. The bars in Figure 7.2a show the extent to which the proportion of "more important" tasks received from a particular source deviates, on average, from the overall average proportion of "more important" tasks that the managers handled. Figure 7.2b shows the same thing for "less important" tasks. A clear hierarchical pattern,

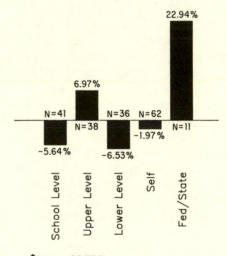

FIG. 7.2a. "More important" rating by source (deviation from mean)*. A manager's ratings of the importance of a particular source were included only if the manager spent at least 5 percent of his or her time responding to that source. Consequently, the averages shown in the figure are based on different N's.

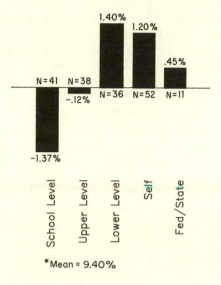

1.40%
1.20%
.45%
N=41   N=38
-.12%   N=36   N=52   N=11
-1.37%

School Level   Upper Level   Lower Level   Self   Fed/State

*Mean = 9.40%

FIG. 7.2b. "Less important" rating by source (deviation from mean)*. A manager's ratings of the importance of a particular source were included only if the manager spent at least 5 percent of his or her time responding to that source. Consequently, the averages shown in the figure are based on different N's.

which we would expect in a system dominated by the social structure, is evident. Tasks from lower-level managers and school-level personnel, and, interestingly enough, self-initiated tasks were not considered as important, on average, as tasks received from upper-level managers and from state and federal officials. Indeed, tasks from state and federal officials, who represent the larger hierarchy in which school districts operate, received the highest importance rating by far.

Upper-level managers rated a higher proportion of tasks in each of these categories "more important" than did lower-level managers, although the pattern of the two groups was similar. Tasks from upper-level managers were rated almost identically by the two groups (33.8 percent by upper; 31.8 percent by lower). Self-initiated tasks, however, were rated differently. Upper-level managers considered their self-initiated tasks "more important" at twice the rate of lower-level managers (34.3 versus 17.7 percent). Upper-level managers might take their own initiatives more seriously for a number of reasons. For example, they might think what they do is important because others think it is important, or because their authority is behind their actions, or because more of their actions are, indeed, consequential. (There is also the possibility that the reason they got ahead in the first place is because they believed in themselves; they behaved *as if* they carry out important work.)

There are two possible reasons for the hierarchical pattern shown in Figure 7.2. The first has already been suggested: because of the ambiguities that surround administrative work, managers look for a concrete basis for judging the importance of a request and the rank of the individual making the request is usually clear enough to provide such a basis. Managers probably assume, as most people do, that higher-ranked individuals handle matters that are of greater value to the organization, so requests that come from the higher ranks tend to be seen as more important, on average, than tasks that come from the lower ranks. A manager's rank, in this view, signals a task's importance. Implicitly, this reasoning assumes that managers strive to perform in the organization's best interest and look for direction on how to proceed. They find this direction in the source of the task.

A second explanation takes the view that an administrative system is basically a political system (Cyert and March 1963; Pfeffer 1981) in which the power and the resources an individual possesses are correlated with rank. Higher-ranked individuals make job assignments, confer status, and award promotions. Federal and state officials dispense grants, set deadlines, and establish rules. It pays to pay attention to these people. They can dole out rewards to those they feel are worthy. "Worthiness" in an administrative system, however, is difficult to measure objectively. So those who want rewards must figure out ways to make themselves valued by those with power. Demonstrating one's value to an individual is easier than demonstrating one's value to the organization. Simply being responsive to another's directive is one way of doing this. Superiors may have a difficult time determining the individual contributions of subordinates; but they do know if subordinates are attentive and timely in their responses to requests. Similarly, upper-level managers may not be able to evaluate the contributions of colleagues, but they would know if the colleagues helped them out when asked. And while upper-level managers might not be in a position to reward colleagues with promotions, they would be in a position at least to pay them back in kind. In such a system where individual output is difficult to judge, rewards are heavily based on the people you know and the impression these people have of you. Impressions and actual contributions, of course, need not be at odds with each other, but neither are they necessarily identical. One cannot help thinking, though, that a system where individuals must be concerned with managing impressions of themselves in order to get ahead operates with built-in inefficiencies in a way that a system where individuals are judged on the basis of their actual contribution would not.[4]

Judging attentiveness to the wishes of a superior is like judging the interaction behavior discussed in previous chapters: managerial action associated with organizational objectives and those with private objectives are hard to distinguish. Indeed, in standard bureaucratic theories, following the directives of superiors is a virtue because it is an important element that contributes to bureaucratic efficiency, assuming that superiors are knowledgeable and know best what subordinates should do. This assumption and therefore the principle of supervision from above, however, are not clear in an administrative system. In fact, we could argue that too heavy a reliance on directives from above could be dysfunctional. There are two reasons why this is so. The first is that important messages coming from other sources could be undervalued or missed altogether. Attention is a fixed resource. If an administrative system is viewed as a problem-solving system, as suggested in chapter 6, then problems, at least operational ones, should flow to the top from lower-level managers who are closer to them. In order for the system to work well those in the lower levels must send the messages, and those in the upper levels must pay serious attention to them. We saw in the preceding chapter, however, that lower-level managers are reluctant to send them. One of the reasons suggested for this reluctance was the cool reception they receive when they do. The findings here provide supporting evidence for this; or at least they suggest that the initiatives of lower-level managers are not generally considered very important by those in higher positions. Lower-level managers no doubt are able to sense this. Upper-level managers probably overvalue and rely too heavily on other upper-level managers for information about what is going on in their organization; and they probably undervalue and do not take seriously information transmitted from lower levels.

I should point out that higher-ranked individuals are not necessarily looking for the special attention they receive. What they do and what they want (or what others think they want) are often taken more seriously by others than they intend them to be. This is the second problem associated with taking cues for action from upper-level managers: they often cause an overreaction. For subordinates, doing something that pleases the boss has the advantage of both giving direction to action in an ambiguous world and putting them in good stead with a dispenser of rewards. Whether or not higher-ranked individuals like it, unless they have done something to lose their credibility, other individuals in the organization are likely to be keenly sensitive, and probably overly attentive, to their actions and preferences. When a new boss takes over a job, for instance, subordinates typically spend many hours hanging on to his or her every word and action and trying to interpret it in a way that will give guidance to their own behavior. A superintendent in a neighboring district to the one I studied, for example, found that some casual remarks she had made about a particular instructional approach almost resulted in a complete overhaul of the in-service teacher training program in her district. What happened was that when she made the rounds of her district to chat informally with and to get to know some of the personnel, she had asked on a number of occasions what a teacher or curriculum supervisor or principal thought about "direct instruction."[5] The superintendent was not an advocate of this approach, but she had recently read some articles on the relative merits of "direct" and "indirect" instruction and she was simply curious about what her professional staff thought about it. Her staff, however, mistook her professional inquisitiveness as a statement or at least a signal of her preferences. Luckily, before the in-service program was redesigned, probably causing hard feelings among those who had originally developed it, the superintendent heard about the plans and put a stop to them. She had to explain that she was not a proponent of "direct" instruction and, in fact, had serious misgivings about it. She also thought that the current in-service program was outstanding. Interestingly enough, she had learned about the plans from the superintendent in the next district who had heard about it in a casual conversation over lunch from his director of in-service programs. Within her own organization, her preferences were not questioned; they were inferred and quickly accepted as guidelines for behavior.

It is not necessarily only superiors who receive special attention; it could also be peers or counterparts. Indeed, it could be any individual who has valued resources or political power. For example, we would expect managers to be particularly attentive to other managers with whom they might form a coalition or with whom they would be involved in bargaining and compromising over organizational decisions. These other managers would mostly tend to be upper-level managers, although those lower in the hierarchy who control critical areas of uncertainty for the organization can have an inordinate amount of power for their position.[6]

There are also reasons, other than power, that managers may pay particularly close attention to those is upper ranks. For example, if the system filters managers well, those who reach the upper ranks are, on average, more competent and probably more able to judge the competence of others than those who do not. And managers, like most people, put out more effort when faced with more competent judges. In addition, even if they have no direct power over another manager, higher-ranked individuals may receive deferential treatment simply because they have higher status.

In general, lacking clear objective measures of marginal output and value, administrative systems work through people's judgments about what and who is good. Interpreting the importance of a task in terms of the rank of its carrier or its source may be as reasonable a way to proceed as any, but as the above discussion suggests, it can also create problems.

Content

The importance ratings of tasks in terms of content show a hierarchical pattern similar to the ratings by source. (See Figure 7.3a.) Those tasks that relate to school-level concerns — the ultimate locus of production in this organization, that is, student issues, parent/community relations, and curriculum issues, received the lowest ratings. Matters that could be defined as strictly manage-

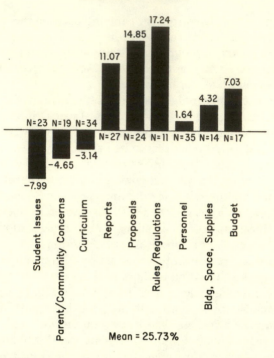

Fɪɢ. 7.3a. "More important" tasks by content (deviations from mean)*. A manager's ratings of the importance of a particular content area were included only if the manager spent at least 5 percent of his or her time on issues in that area. Consequently, the averages shown in the figure are based on different N's.

ment concerns, that is, personnel; building, space, and supplies; and budget, received moderate ratings, and issues that relate mainly to the management of external relations, that is, reports, proposals, and regulations, were rated highest in terms of importance. With the exception of budget items, tasks concerned with proposals and regulations were also the least likely to be considered "less" important. (See Figure 7.3b.)

In this section I describe these patterns and suggest reasons for them. I discuss the dominance of tasks that relate to external relations further in chapter 8.

Belief in the importance of tasks concerned with external rela-

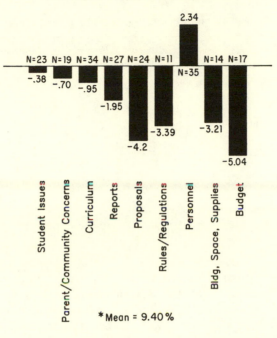

FIG. 7.3b. "Less important" tasks by content (deviations from mean)*. A manager's ratings of the importance of a particular content area were included only if the manager spent at least 5 percent of his or her time on issues in that area. Consequently, the averages shown in the figure are based on different N's.

tions and external resources pervades the organization. The general order of these ratings holds even for managers whose primary responsibility is the regular school program and who officially have little to do with external relations or with externally funded programs (Hannaway 1985a). Table 7.1 compares the rankings of managers who were responsible for federal and state categorical programs with the rankings of managers who had no responsibility for externally funded programs and whose jobs were formally defined as providing assistance to school-level personnel on curriculum and teaching concerns. Categorical program managers most often rated tasks concerned with program reports, regulations, and proposals as "more important." This is not surprising; dealing with such mat-

TABLE 7.1   Importance Rankings of Task Content

	Categorical Program Managers	Instructional Liaison Managers
Curriculum	5	8
Student issues	7	7
Parent/community relations	8	6
Budget	4	5
Personnel	6	4
Proposal development	2	3
Report preparation	1	2
Rules/regulations	3	1

ters is their primary function, and it is, in fact, the way they spend most of their time.[7] However, it is surprising that the ratings of the instructional liaison managers are so similar. The primary function of these managers is working with teachers and principals on curriculum and instruction, and yet these tasks were the least likely to be considered important. In fact, they spend a very small fraction of their time on categorical aid programs.[8]

Handling tasks related to external funding may not only be considered important work by managers; it may also be the preferred work in the organization. This work presents special opportunities for managers. The relationship between the power of an actor in an organization and the actor's ability to cope with critical organizational uncertainties has been noted by a number of researchers (Pfeffer 1981; Hickson et al. 1981; Crozier 1964). External funds represent critical contingencies for the organization, so establishing good relationships with external agents and being viewed as handling externally funded programs adeptly could have direct implications for the amount of power an individual can wield in the organization.[9]

It may seem surprising that categorical aid programs commanded such serious attention from managers since they do not represent a large proportion of the total resources of the school district; in fact, they represent only about 11 percent of the budget. But, although the total amounts are relatively small, they represent the only part of the budget that is not allocated by standard procedures. Personnel costs, for example, which represent about 80 percent of a school district's expenditures, are determined mainly by union negotiation and local norms of class size. The allocation of categorical program budgets, in contrast, can be significantly affected by the actions of individual managers. Title I programs, for example, which are the largest federally funded programs, are designed locally. Federal regulations target the funds to needy student populations, but local districts determine the ways in which that population will be served. Categorical program resources thus represent an area over which a manager can exercise, or appear to exercise, considerable influence, and this can translate into tremendous power in the organization (Pfeffer 1981). This has been referred to as the "10% rule," "which states that organizations can be taken over by discretionary control over not more than (and frequently much less than) 10% of the organization's total budget" (Pfeffer 1981,106). Managers with connections to the outside may be highly valued by others in the organization for another reason. As I have mentioned a number of times in this book, managers are often uncertain how to value something or someone because there are no objective standards. In these situations the opinions of others may weigh especially heavily. Outsiders are viewed, perhaps, as independent and therefore more objective judges.

Tasks that related to the "production" concerns in the organization, such as teaching and learning, were the least likely to be considered very important. Such a low rating of production tasks may be peculiar to educational organizations where — as in most human service organizations — the technology associated with production is not well understood. Both the critical factors that affect student learning and the ways they interact with different students at different times are abstruse for a variety of reasons. It is difficult for a manager to generate noticeable returns for efforts in this direction. In fact, getting too heavily involved in teaching and learning may cause resentment by some teachers who consider this their professional arena. It could also be argued that education is a field with low prestige and that tasks associated with it also have low prestige; tasks that relate more directly to management have higher prestige, which makes them more attractive to managers and gives them greater satisfaction.

The high level of importance attached to tasks concerned with external relations and the low level of importance attached to tasks concerned with teaching and learning turn on its head a view of managers as facilitators whose function is to serve the "production" part of the organization so it can do its job better. These ratings of importance are more compatible with the view that the function of management is not so much to serve or to direct the central core of the organization, but rather to buffer it (Thompson 1967) and legitimize it to the outside world (Meyer and Rowan 1977; DiMaggio and Powell 1983).

Activity

Chapters 4 and 5 showed that managers in my study spent the vast majority of their time in interactions—21 percent in large group meetings, 10 percent in meetings with three to four individuals, 23 percent in one-to-one meetings, and 10 percent on the telephone. It was suggested in chapter 5 that, in a sense, a large group meeting could be viewed as a "sink." More and more managers could be added to meetings and kept busy with little, if any, noticeable beneficial impact on the organization. But the findings here indicate that managers generally considered those interaction activities that included a large number of people to be highly important. (See Figure 7.4a.) On average they placed more than a third of their large group meetings (34.5 percent) in the "more important" category. Why?

It is hard to imagine that the typical or "average" large meeting has very high productivity. It is even harder to imagine that the marginal meeting makes much difference; or, more specifically, that the marginal contribution of additional managers to most of these meetings is significant. One possible explanation for why managers rated these meetings highly is that they provided opportunities to disseminate important information and generate discussion on important issues. Another explanation is that these are symbolic gatherings whose primary function is to promote a sense of community which is valued in and of itself. Perhaps they are the grease that kept the wheels of the system moving, and the managers may have recognized this. A third explanation is that managers used the number of individuals in attendance as a signal of importance: if they are investing so much in this meeting, they must be doing something very important.

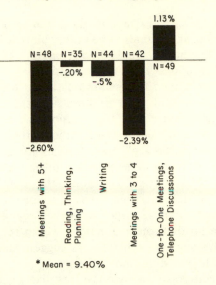

Fig. 7.4a. "More important" rating by activity (deviations from mean)*.
A manager's ratings of importance of a particular activity were included
only if the manager spent at least 5 percent of his or her time on that
activity.

A fourth explanation is compatible with the view that administrative organizations are people-dominated political systems where who's who and who's there is important. A large group meeting is a forum where managers can persuade each other of their views and convince each other of their worth; where they can publicly display and legitimize their power. It is probably the best setting for managing general impressions in the organization and also for collecting information on who has power and what they think is important. It is also a place where managers can demonstrate that they are members of the team. In the absence of more substantive measures of worth, participating in these formal displays of community can be very important.

Whatever the reasons, managers do not view these meetings as a waste of time. Both upper- and lower-level managers considered large meetings "less important" less often than average (8.1 percent and 6.1 percent, respectively). (See Figure 7.4b.) In fact, upper-level managers considered them more important than did lower-level managers. Upper-level managers considered 41.8 percent of the meetings with more than five individuals and 45.6 percent of those with three to four individuals to be in the "more important" category. Lower-level managers rated 30.5 percent and 28.3 percent of the same types of meetings "more important."

Remember that these ratings are relative to what the managers "usually do." In general, these findings suggest that at least upper-level managers consider public persuasion and public displays of power very important. As suggested earlier in the book, large meetings may be "broadcasting" opportunities for them. Lower-level managers also consider large meetings to be very important, but perhaps for a different reason. Although they may attempt to demonstrate their worth in these meetings, they can also find out what is currently valued by those in power in the organization. Unfortunately, I have no data on interactions within these meetings, although small group research findings suggest that they would be dominated by higher-status individuals.

Telephone conversations were the least likely activity to be considered very important. Managers do not convey or collect important information this way, which makes sense. A telephone call is

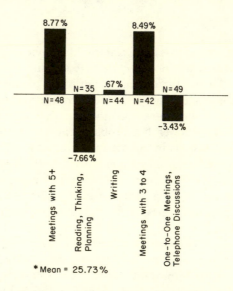

Fig.7.4b. "Less important" rating by activity (deviations from mean)*. A manager's ratings of importance of a particular activity were included only if the manager spent at least 5 percent of his or her time on that activity.

not very costly either for the sender or the receiver — it is certainly less costly and less intrusive than a meeting. Since it is spontaneous, it requires no set-up costs. And because managers make and receive telephone calls right in their offices, there are no "transportation" costs. Managers probably also feel less need for social pleasantries over the phone than they do in person, so they can come to the point and transact their business more quickly.[10] Telephones provide managers with a quick and easy way to dispense with unimportant matters so they can move on to other things.

Reading is another activity that received a low importance rating. Managers do not collect important information by reading; they deal with important matters face to face. As suggested earlier in the book, written material is probably for the record and not for the transmission of information. "Planning" and "thinking" were included in the same response category as "reading," and one would have expected these to boost the importance rating of this category. But they did not. Why? Managers clearly do not view planning and thinking as unimportant activities! There are two possible reasons for the low rating. First, managers might have done so little planning and thinking that they did not affect the overall importance rating of the category; or, second, as I discuss in chapter 3, planning is not a behavioral activity of managers, so that when "real" planning went on it fell within another category, such as meetings. Planning is not something that occurs in ivory tower isolation. Managers think and plan aloud, and they typically do it interactively. In fact, Lee Iacocca (1984) credits his success to this form of planning: "The best way to *develop* an idea is through interacting with your fellow managers. . . . It's been a big part of my own success, . . . I'm a great believer in having executives spend time together talking — not always in formal meetings but simply shooting the breeze, helping each other out, and solving problems" (p. 59).

In addition to large meetings, tasks that involved writing were also considered important. This is compatible with the view expressed in chapter 4 that, because written material leaves a record and provides evidence in a fairly permanent form, managers take what they write especially seriously. The contrast between reading and writing is an interesting one. What is written is important to the author; he or she may be judged by it at some future time. But it is not important to the reader, who expects important information to come in person.

Implications for the Working of Administrative Systems

The study findings described in this chapter showed a clear relationship between the rank of the carrier of a task and the importance that is attached to that task by others. This suggests that the carriers of tasks have considerable influence on how the work in the system is carried out. Specifically, they affect the intensity or seriousness with which managers engage in their work. This has a number of implications for how administrative systems function. A task directed by, or perhaps even suggested by, an upper-level manager will receive special attention by others in the organization. In fact, it may receive more attention than the upper-level management thinks appropriate. This is problematic because requests that are considered "more important" will probably "bump" whatever else managers might be working on when they receive them, and upper-level managers are probably unaware both of the seriousness that will be given to their requests and also of what they might be "bumping." Their requests receive priority treatment, but the opportunity costs for handling their tasks are not known, either by the upper-level managers who diverted attention or by the individuals who responded. The same holds for requests in this organization by state and federal officials. Given the responsiveness to directives from upper-level managers, it may be a good thing for administrative systems that upper-level managers directly control only a small proportion of the work of lower managers. Upper-level managers could probably do much damage to the routine operation of the system . . . and probably not even know they were doing it.

If carriers influence the importance attached to issues, then this influence has direct implications for how to change the focus of a system. For example, a major reform movement in education is currently underway in the United States. School districts have been exhorted to pay more serious attention to what, and how much, students are learning. The findings here suggest that exhortations may not be sufficient. Upper-level managers themselves may have to focus their own attention directly on teaching and learning concerns and to be the direct carriers of these issues to others. They may have to get out of their offices and get involved in the school's tasks. And, indeed, research on schools has shown that if principals demonstrate active involvement in teaching and learning concerns, schools are more effective. (See, for example, Shoemaker and Fraser 1981.) Popular accounts of successful managers report something similar: They get involved in a "hands-on" way with production or with the services offered by their firms (Peters and Waterman 1982). In these cases, managers may not be contributing to productivity directly, but they are probably having a significant indirect effect by giving a sense of seriousness to certain tasks. Their actions and involvement are symbolic. Indeed, Peters and Waterman argue that "symbols are the very stuff of management behavior. Executives, after all, do not synthesize chemicals or operate lift trucks; they deal in symbols" (1982,10).

While the symbolic identification of upper-level management with certain tasks may have a significant effect on the involvement and seriousness of other actors, large group meetings seem to convey their own importance. They are the ceremonies in which meanings and interpretations of events are transmitted and in which the power of various actors is legitimized. They are considered very important events by all managers.

The importance attached to large meetings has implications for the growth of these systems. As you will recall from chapter 5, calling these meetings is very costly for the organization in terms of managerial time because of their multiplier effects. This chapter shows that managers consider large meetings to be highly important and are probably eager to attend them, which makes it extremely easy to call them, probably too easy. In fact, managers may encourage each other to call meetings in subtle ways, for example, by their willingness to attend them. This no doubt varies by setting. In systems where productivity and an individual's contribution to it is clearer, resistance to attending many group meetings is probably greater. But in settings where individual output is less clear, managers should watch time spent in large meetings carefully.

NOTES

1. This measure assumes that managers are more involved with, pay closer attention to, and generally expend more effort on tasks they feel are important (Greenwald 1981; Greenwald and Leavitt 1984).

2. It is difficult to evaluate the significance of the differences between the results obtained from the upper- and lower-level managers. They could

indicate a number of things. It is possible, for example, that the assessments accurately represent the distribution of tasks at different levels. Upper-level managers could, in fact, deal with more "more important" issues and more "less important" issues; that is, there is higher variance in their work than in the work of lower-level managers. Alternatively, it might indicate differences in the quality of managers at different levels. The distribution of important tasks may be the same at both levels; but upper-level managers are better discriminators of a task's importance, a qualitative difference that perhaps has been recognized and rewarded by promotion in the organization.

3. I report source, activity, and content separately. Each of these factors has an independent and statistically significant effect on managers' ratings of task importance. In a maximum likelihood logit model using a random sample of tasks ($N=3750$) the t-statistics associated with source, activity, and content were 7.1, 8.1, and 9.7, respectively.

4. This begs the question, of course, of whether there are alternative organizational designs that could alleviate these inefficiencies given the problems of uncertainty and ambiguity in administrative systems.

5. Direct instruction refers to a set of behavioral principles for instruction. This type of instruction is mostly teacher-directed, and materials are highly structured. (See Rosenshine 1979 and Peterson 1979 for a fuller explanation.)

6. Crozier (1964), for example, found that the maintenance workers in a plant he studied had an enormous amount of power in spite of their relatively low hierarchical status. Their power was based on their ability to repair the machinery, which was the only area of uncertainty in an otherwise completely routinized process. Mechanic (1962) has noted other sources of power for lower-level participants in organizations.

7. Categorical aid program managers spent only 4 percent of their time on the regular school program. See Hannaway (1985a).

8. Division of Instruction managers who were not directly responsible for categorical aid programs spent 8.8 percent of their time on these programs. See Hannaway (1985a).

9. It is interesting that the director of federal and state programs went on to become the superintendent of the school district.

10. Electronic mail will probably replace the use of telephones for transmitting spontaneous and not very important information in the future. It is even less intrusive than the telephone and has the additional advantage that no one has to be physically present to receive messages; they can be stored. However, electronic messages will probably be more highly edited than phone information because managers are more careful about what they put in writing.

8

What If . . . ?

The preceding chapters described the behavior of managers on the job and tried to make sense of it. This chapter builds on the thinking presented earlier and considers the consequences of changes in the structure of the system and changes in the demands on the system from the external environment. I attempt to predict how the system might function differently as a consequence of these changes.

Structural Changes

Organizations change shape over time. They may bulge in the middle, be top-heavy, lopsided, or quite streamlined. Sometimes shapes result from conscious design decisions, such as much of the restructuring currently underway in major corporations. At other times shapes result from multiple pressures, such as the independent hiring and firing decisions of an organizational unit and the quit decisions of individuals, which occur over a long period without anyones being really aware of the overall shape being produced. Although most of the literature on organizational structure has been concerned with the determinants of structure,[1] my interest here is with the *effect* of organizational structure, specifically its effect on managerial work patterns in an administrative system.[2] How does structure affect how administrative work is carried out?

While there are a number of dimensions of organizational structure that might affect the behavior of managers, I consider only two particular kinds of structural changes here. The first is a proportionate increase in the number of managers at a given level — whether it is upper or middle, and lower. The second is increased horizontal differentiation in the form of specialization.

Increase in the Upper Ranks

According to classical bureaucratic theory, an increase in the relative number of upper-level managers, other things not changing, would have two major effects. First, the monitoring and supervising capacity of the system would be enlarged so that upper-level managers would be able to exercise tighter control over the operations of the organization and be generally better informed about its goings on. The second effect partly flows from the first: the quality of decisions would be increased because a larger number of upper-level managers would mean that the number of sensors collecting information relevant to both the strategic and operational needs of the organization would be increased.

According to the ideas and findings of chapter 5, however, the effects of increasing the number of upper-level managers would be different from those predicted by classical theory. One likely effect, for example, would be the increased isolation of the top. The larger the relative number of upper-level managers, the more isolated they would become from the rest of the organization. Although upper-level managers tend to interact heavily with each other, they are not very responsive to organizational members outside their rank. Whether we interpret importance ratings in terms of preferences (i.e., managers would prefer to do more of the things they think are important and less of the things they think are unimportant) or in terms of "pressure" (i.e., that managers feel more pressed to respond to demands they think are important than to demands they think are less important), upper-level managers respond to the increase in demands made by additional upper-level managers at the expense of other demands.

Many of the additional demands among upper-level managers would represent necessary coordination costs that simply come with greater numbers. Upper-level managers, for example, are typically assigned a sphere of responsibility that must be coordinated with others in order for concerted organizational action. The more spheres to coordinate, the greater the costs. Other demands are simply acknowledgments of the participation rights of upper-level managers, who typically work as a team; and the number of areas in which a manager has participation rights increases with rank (Cohen, March, and Olsen 1972). Consequently, higher-ranked managers receive a broader range and higher volume of communications and are invited to a greater number of meetings. In general, additional upper-level managers would intensify the communication demands and coordination costs within the upper ranks, which most likely would result in weakening the connection of senior managers to others, particularly lower-level managers and production people (in the case I studied, school-level administrators and teachers).

Given the "pack" tendencies of upper-level managers, an increase in the number of managers at this level would at some point result in an overall loss of informational efficiency within the organization. The volume of interaction among top managers would increase, but the value of the information received could decrease.[3] The information channels among those in the upper level, where much of the information is probably redundant, would be widened, while the information channels from the lower levels, where the information presumably has more real value, would be narrowed. Indeed, the predicted effects of increasing upper-management ranks, *ceteris paribus*, runs counter to the view that "the aim in designing institutions for making decisions should be to facilitate the flow of information to the greatest extent possible. . . . [T]his involves the reduction of the volume of information while preserving as much of its value as possible" (Arrow 1974,70).

Another effect of adding more upper-level managers could be increased innovation in the system. Upper-level managers are likely (at least more likely than lower-level managers) to initiate nonroutine work on their own, which would also intensify work in the upper ranks for two reasons. The higher the volume of uncertain tasks upper-level managers handle the more they interact, and they primarily interact with each other. In addition, as chapter 7 indicated, since they take uncertain tasks very seriously they would tend to be very involved in them.

At some point an increased number of upper-level managers would lead to further structural differentiation within the system. The information-sharing and joint decision-making costs would become so great that the participation rights of managers would have to be altered. Different managers would have access to different areas of decision making, and a system with more specialized units would emerge. Coordination needs would increase, and an additional hierarchical level would probably be introduced to fulfill that function. What before looked like a team would look more and more like a hierarchy, and the resulting structure would affect interaction patterns in predictable ways. Connections that had been strong among upper-level managers would be weakened because, as I showed in chapter 6, hierarchical distinctions induce information distortions; managers send information up the hierarchy selectively.

Managerial systems are more prone to hierarchical elaboration than production systems. The reason for this is that the higher one is placed in an organization the less restricted are the rights and responsibilities of the job. As chapter 5 showed, managers working with neither performance directives nor performance standards get easily overloaded; the job is never clearly defined and never done. One common solution to the problem is hiring more managers, which was discussed earlier. Another solution would be restructuring the system in an attempt to define job specialties and to restrict some of the demands. Both solutions would at some point result in additional hierarchical levels.

The effect of adding lower-level managers would be less dramatic than adding upper-level managers. Demands within the system would no doubt increase, but lower-level initiatives are not taken very seriously by other managers. Other managers, particularly upper-level managers, can decide how seriously to attend to, or not to attend to, initiatives from lower levels. If we are guided by the importance ratings in chapter 7, lower-level demands may not generate much response from other managers. The time of managers is fixed and they seem to prefer to direct their attention in other ways.

Lower-level managers also tend to be conservative. Because they are far more likely to stick to the routine aspects of their work than to undertake nonroutine tasks, they would not tend to "get in people's hair" and cause problems. The supervisory demands created when an additional lower-level manager undertakes mainly routine work are small, so that the pressure for a structural change, specifically an additional hierarchical level, produced by an additional lower-level manager would be small — certainly considerably smaller than the pressure created by an additional upper-level manager who would introduce more nonroutine work into the system. The large number of studies showing that span of control is inversely related to task uncertainty supports this view (Galbraith 1977).

Horizontal Differentiation: Specialization

Increased specialization is another structural change (which I mentioned briefly earlier as a likely consequence of additional upper-level managers). Specialization alleviates pressure created by uncertainty and complexity by restricting the range of tasks that managers must handle. Presumably, specialization is also more efficient locally. Because managers handle a narrower range of tasks, their experience expertise in handling those tasks increase.

My data suggest that specialization might have another effect: it increases the involvement of managers with particular types of tasks, or at least it seems to affect the involvement of the upper-level managers who are directly responsible for those tasks. Managers give more serious attention to their area of specialization. Table 8.1 shows the proportion of tasks rated "more important" by man-

TABLE 8.1   Specialization and Importance Ratings

Manager	Task Category	% More Important	Average Rating of Other Managers[a]
Associate Superintendent for Instruction	Curriculum	67	20[b]
Deputy for Instruction	Curriculum	52	20[c]
Federal/State Liaison	Reports	86	35[d]
Comptroller	Budget	66	31[e]

[a]Only the ratings of managers who spent more than 5 percent of their time in the content area were included.
[b]$N = 32$
[c]$N = 32$
[d]$N = 26$
[e]$N = 16$

agers in charge of specialized areas. They show, for example, the rating of budget tasks by the comptroller; the ratings of the associate superintendent of instruction and his deputy for curriculum tasks, and the ratings of the federal/state program liaison for reports. The table also shows the average proportion of tasks in that category rated "more important" by all the managers.

Thus, one way to direct more serious attention to specific matters is to create specialized positions for dealing with them. This arrangement will probably at least affect the involvement of upper-level managers[4] who, in turn, can affect the involvement of lower-level managers by sending them tasks directly. The benefits of increased specialization, of course, have to be balanced against inevitable increases in coordination costs.

Environmental Changes

It is commonly recognized that an organization's context has important effects on its actions and structure. (See Pfeffer and Salancik 1978; Aldrich 1979; and Meyer and Scott 1983 for reviews.) The findings in chapter 7 support this idea that the external environment of an organization affects its internal processes. It does this through a direct effect on the allocations of attention and effort of individual managers. Indeed, the finding that managers rated tasks associated with external relations "more important" more often than any other type of task suggests that what goes on outside the organization affects what goes on inside in a very significant way. In chapter 7 I used importance ratings to indicate the level of involvement of managers with various tasks, but if managers prefer or feel compelled to respond to tasks that they think are important before tasks that they think are not important, external demands will take precedence over other demands. Thus, an increase in the level of demands from the outside would have definite implications for the workings of the system.

I suggested a number of reasons in chapter 7 for the importance managers attach to tasks that relate to external relations. Certainly, a basic reason is that external demands are objectively important; they represent real constraints that must be satisfied in order for the organization to receive resources necessary for its survival. Because of this dependence, organizational members spend considerable effort dealing with environmental contingencies in order to ensure a continual flow of resources. (See, for example, Pfeffer and Salancik 1978 for discussion.) And the greater the need for some particular resource and the more limited the availability of alternative suppliers of that resource, the greater importance managers attach to external demands from the provider of that resource. The types of resources providers contribute to an organization vary with the type of organization. For example, they may include direct payments from customers for products received or from clients for services rendered, tax support, or support in the form of goodwill and legitimacy (Scott 1981).

But not all external demands may be as important to the organization as managers perceive them to be. In fact if managers are risk averse, as I discussed in chapter 4, we would expect them to overrate and overreact to external demands, because there is a chance that the organization (and/or its participants) can be made much worse off if external agents feel dissatisfaction (which does not necessarily mean that the organization can be made much better off as a consequence of managerial efforts). Bad external relations are certainly something to avoid, but managers invest more heavily than is perhaps necessary in managing their external dependencies. Keeping resource providers more than satisfied, say by being more responsive to them than necessary and by providing more information than requested, is like stockpiling inventory; only in this case managers are stockpiling good will. Stockpiles protect the organization from forces that are outside its control and are often unpredictable. In a public organization, they reduce the likelihood both of questions from the outside and of close monitoring by outside agents of the organization's operation. Good public relations provide "cover" for the organization, but the fraction of effort that is over and above what is necessary to keep resources flowing into the organization represents slack in the system's operation.

In the organization I studied, the chances of, say, losing funding from either state or federal officials were in fact quite small (although not zero). Most of the funding was done through entitlement formulas (based on client characteristics) and thus was not tied to the performance of the school district. Not returning phone calls promptly and preparing reports a bit less thoroughly would rarely have affected the amount of funding significantly. But managers attended to them very seriously, probably because they believed that catering to resource providers was likely to ward off possible problems.

The relative importance of any particular task associated with external demands is probably difficult to distinguish very accurately. But managers do know that external tasks are generally important. The rule they seem to follow is: If it is an external matter, take it seriously. It is an easy rule to follow, but it generally results in management's overinvestment in external relations.

The special handling of external relations is probably nowhere clearer than in the way federal agencies treat even routine requests for information from congressional offices, especially if the member of Congress making the request is on one of the committees charged with overseeing the agency. When these requests are received in the agency, they typically get "flagged," logged in, and processed under clearance procedures and stringent deadlines. The turnaround time for these requests is often under twenty-four hours, even though the vast majority of them are not very important in terms of the overall objectives of the agency. A congressman's request may be concerned with, say, a minor calculation error in the veteran's benefits of one individual. But because the congressman made the request, and the agency's authorization and appropriations are dependent upon congressional action, the request is treated as if it were very important, bumping whatever else is on the manager's desk. What concerns the agency, first and foremost, is not as much tending to the issue involved in the task as it is keeping in the good graces of a resource provider, a quite separate objective.

Managers also do not want to risk their own well-being. Of all the problems they deal with, they are probably least likely to take chances with external relations. They know that problems, when they are visible, send off alarms in the organization and invite close scrutiny of associated managers and their actions. Important problems — resource problems — that might threaten part of the organization's lifeline, are "three alarmers" that surely will single managers out for surveillance. This is clearly something managers want to avoid for their own good; they want to protect their areas of discretion just as organizations want to protect their independence. Self-protection provides another reason why managers pay particularly close attention to external relations and why external relations tasks can easily contribute to slack in management's operation.

As discussed in chapter 7, external demands also represent opportunities for managers to demonstrate their abilities. Power, for example, accrues to managers who are viewed as handling critical contingencies for the organization. A smart manager who has established good relations with officials in a funding agency can wield considerable power in the organization, especially if no one else in the system has established the same contacts. The payoff for handling external relations well is probably considerably greater than the payoffs associated with good work in other areas of management responsibility.

If the above view is correct, an increase in external demands from resource providers would have a disproportionate effect on the allocation of managerial time and attention in two ways. First, because managers consider external relations tasks to be very important (or the most important) for both private and organizational reasons, few of these tasks (opportunities) would pass by them unnoticed. Thus, the ratio of demands taken up by managers to demands presented to them would probably be greatest for external relations tasks. Second, when actually performing the tasks, managers would probably give them more time and pay closer attention to them than necessary because there are private gains, in addition to organizational benefits, to be obtained from handling them well and serious negative consequences for mishandling them. Similarly, a decrease in external demands would have a disproportionate effect; managers would probably reduce their attention to these matters less than the demands actually required. In fact, one study showed that even after the federal government reduced reporting requirements, education administrators persisted in submitting lengthy proposals and extensive evaluations (Hastings 1983).

I should note that the clients of the organization I studied — parents and community members — are not included in this discussion of resource providers even though a large share of organizational revenues come from local taxes. In fact, tasks that directly concerned these resource providers were considered among the least important. One reason, perhaps the main reason, is that taxpayers or clients have very little clout as individuals. The source of resources for local public agencies is typically not concentrated; it is spread over thousands of taxpayers. Unless taxpayers are organized, their demands do not have to be taken very seriously . . . and they do not seem to be. The position of customers of firms is similar. It is very difficult for a dissatisfied customer to get, say, General Motors to pay much attention to him. The demands of state and federal agents are taken seriously because the resources controlled by state and federal agencies are concentrated and there are no real alternative providers. Consequently, state and federal agents have clout.

In the examples I have given, investing effort in external relations is often a strategy of risk aversion, not one of entrepreneurship. This may be less likely in private organizations, than in public organizations, where the bounds of legitimate managerial objectives and managerial activities are more circumscribed and the set of external actors that have to be satisfied is greater. Those who pay for public services are often not those who benefit. An entrepreneurial activity in a public organization that might please one group might very well generate conflict with another.

As far as both the organization and the manager are concerned, the costs of handling external relations tasks well are sometimes less clear than the benefits. Managerial time and attention are limited. If managers invest their time and energies more heavily in one area, something else has to "give." If we assume that those activities that would "give" would be those that managers consider least important, then in the organization I studied these would be curriculum and student issues — the core activities, the central production tasks — of the school district. These activities would also include tasks that were concerned with parent and community relations. The implications are obvious. The more demands external agencies place on school districts, the less attention managers will give to production concerns and the concerns of clients.

Is this a pattern we would expect in all types of organizations? The answer is yes, but probably not to the same extent. As I mentioned earlier, every organization must respond to the demands of external resource providers in order to survive. Changing financial markets, for example, require the close attention of executives in financial institutions. But the extent to which, and the ease with which, external relations tasks "bump" internal production tasks varies across different types of organizations. Let me explain.

Organizational actors are more vulnerable to influence when their behaviors or accomplishments are observable. Public behaviors, for example, are more easily influenced than private behaviors (Kiesler and Kiesler 1969). Now consider the demands that external resource providers made of the organization I studied. Because direct observation of school district behavior is impossible, in large part because the system is highly decentralized, external agencies often demand reports, which are visible products. Recall that in chapter 7 one of the tasks that managers considered "more important" was report preparation. Dealing with students, curriculum modification, or other education production tasks does not generally produce a visible outcome, especially in the short run, so managers do not seem to pay particularly close attention to them, and it would be difficult to influence them to do so. In an organization that produced a different product, one where the outcomes of different behaviors (or the behaviors themselves) were more visible, this might not be as true. Closer attention to marketing, for example, could have very visible short-term effects in the sale of some products, and closer attention to production processes might yield some quickly observable efficiencies.

Visibility of outcome is, of course, directly related to accountability and the assignment of costs — costs to the manager and costs to the organization. If the effects of not giving much attention to, say, curriculum are not observable, then the manager cannot be held accountable for them even though neglect of this area may have a detrimental effect on the organization's long-run performance. The effects of curriculum neglect are the opportunity costs of managers' spending their time, say, in external relations. In fact, managers are less likely to incur either the costs or the benefits from tasks with less visible outcomes; the organization does. However, if managers engage in tasks that produce visible outcomes, there are private gains (the manager gets credit) as well as any gains that the organization might receive. There are also risks. And so, in general, we would expect managers to prefer tasks that provide them with private benefits over tasks that do not, but we would also expect them to engage in these tasks cautiously, as I discussed in chapter 4. When external relations are going smoothly, a manager tends to carry them alone; but, as soon as it gets rocky, other managers quickly become involved. Better decisions for the organization might result from this involvement; and, in addition, the manager in these situations would be better off personally sharing the risk.

Yet regardless of the organization's product, maintaining good external relations and ensuring the continual flow of resources to the organization is, as discussed above, absolutely essential for any organization's survival, and tasks associated with this objective will always be considered important by managers responsible for the organization's well-being. The extent to which managers overinvest in external relations will be, to a significant degree, a function of the relative visibility of the behaviors and outcomes associated with external relations and with other management areas of responsibility.

NOTES

1. The largest part of this literature has focused on the effect of environmental conditions and technological factors on the structure of the organization. It argues that the most appropriate structure for an organization depends on characteristics of the environmental and technological demands it faces. The implicit assumption in this literature is that the organization, qua organization, is striving for efficiency. (See Scott, 1975, for a review.) Others stress the importance of strategic choice in producing an organization's structure. In addition to efficiency, choices about appropriate structures reflect other managerial objectives, such as autonomy, stability, and power (Child 1972). More recently, others have stressed the relationship between an organization's structure and the larger normative and institutional environment in which it resides. (See Meyer and Scott 1983; DiMaggio and Powell 1983.)

2. Williamson (1975) has considered the effect of structure, specifically the effect of the M-form structure, on organizational efficiency.

3. Of course if there were reasonably high rates of turnover within the top group, in Pareto's terms if there were a "circulation of elites," informational efficiency might actually be enhanced since the new members would have both new information and easy access to other upper-level managers. But high turnover among upper-level managers is usually unlikely unless there is a general "housecleaning" due to a disaster. Even if there were turnover, information about lower-level operations would probably still prove to be a blind spot.

4. The average rating of other managers in the Division of Instruction (excluding the associate superintendent and his deputy) was 23 percent, only slightly above other managers in general.

9

Putting It Together

This book analyzed the behavior of individual managers at work in an administrative system where there were neither clear guidelines nor unambiguous feedback to direct their behavior. By uncovering and interpreting patterns and processes by which individual managers carry out their work, it identified how the behaviors of individuals combine to produce the behavior of the system—how the micro translates into the macro.

In many ways, this book is probably more aptly described as an interpretative essay than an empirical study. The empirical results provided a point of departure in presenting the view that organizational behavior results from the combined interplay of a number of individual managers who are "boundedly rational" and exist within a hierarchical social system that is characterized by uncertain tasks, ambiguous outcomes, and biased feedback. In this chapter, I sketch out the basic elements of this view and then discuss how it sheds light on three questions that have continually puzzled organizational analysts: Why are organizations conservative? Why do administrative systems grow? Why is "putting out fires" one of a manager's main functions?

An organization acts through the combined actions of the individuals in it. Without people, an organization is, at most, some rooms and some files. Individuals' actions, however, are conditioned by the context in which they operate. Managers at work are not at a party and not at war. The context in which they function is an organization, specifically an administrative system, with a number of characteristics that affect how managers carry out their daily activities. For one thing, every managerial system is almost invariably a *hierarchy*. Some managers are senior to others, but each manager knows his or her place in that hierarchy as well as the place of most other actors. A manager's position in the hierarchy, however, is not fixed. Upward mobility is possible, and most managers prefer to be in a higher rather than in a lower position. Managerial systems are also characterized by *uncertainty* and *ambiguity*. Managers cannot predict very accurately the effects of their actions, and even after the fact, these effects are sometimes not clear partly because the environment in which they work — the actors, the problems, and the solutions facing the organization — is dynamic in unpredictable ways. A corollary of this is that objective measures of a manager's performance are generally not available. Managerial output is difficult to identify even in the aggregate, and the marginal contribution of an individual manager is nearly impossible to factor out.

Managers carry out their work under these conditions of uncertainty and ambiguity. They typically work hard and confront a broad range of daily demands. But they do more than simply respond to stimuli. Managers try to make sense of their world and interpret their environment in ways that will give meaning to their actions. However, because the number of stimuli available exceeds their capacity to handle them, they focus on things selectively and sequentially; that is, they are *boundedly rational*. What they can attend to at any one time is limited. While Simon has not identified what managers attend to and what they do not, he has argued quite forcefully that realistic models of human behavior must take "the bottleneck of attention" into account (Simon 1985). (See chapter 1.) The attention patterns of managers determine managerial actions, and managerial actions are the bases of organizational action.

Two sets of objectives, I argue, underlie a significant part of what managers do. First, most managers try to do a "good job" for the organization. Like most people, they want to have pride in what they do. Second, they want to "get ahead," or, perhaps more importantly, not to be the "fall guy" when things do not turn out well. Behavior that is in the *interest of the organization* and behavior that is in the *interest of the manager*, however do not necessarily coincide. But controlling or restricting privately motivated managerial behavior is very difficult, mainly because it is nearly impossible to distinguish, either by observation or by output, behavior that is in the organization's interest and behavior that is in the private interest of the manager. For example, managers spend the majority of their time interacting with others. No doubt some of this time reflects efforts to define organizational problems and to identify reasonable solutions, but not all of it. Some of it reflects efforts on the part of managers to share responsibilities for various actions; and some of it no doubt reflects managers' efforts to project themselves as knowledgeable and skillful individuals.

Managers are not really sure how to behave in ways that will achieve their objectives—most generally, to make themselves and their organizations better off, or at least not to make themselves worse off. Connections between managerial actions and outcomes are not tight. Managers look for and find cues or signals to give them direction. This is half the story. The other half is that, because managers are motivated in part by their own career interests, and because they know that objective measures of their contributions are not generally available, they not only receive signals, they also send them. They behave in ways that signal their worth to others. In addition, and perhaps most importantly, they try to reduce the likelihood that negative signals are sent about them.

Managers receive cues or signals about what they should do and how seriously they should attend to various aspects of their work from a number of sources. Three of these sources, the social structure, the setting, and external relations, are discussed below. In general, using cues from these sources to direct attention makes good sense from the point of view of the organization. Managers quickly learn what they should attend to for the good of the organization. But because managers are interested in their own welfare as well, they also quickly learn how to manipulate these signals in ways that make them, as individuals, better off.

Managers receive cues from the *social structure* about what to do on the job. Requests for action from higher-ranked managers, for example, are taken very seriously, much more seriously than requests for action from lower-ranked managers. Giving especially serious attention to requests from above generally makes good sense . . . assuming upper-ranked managers are more knowledgeable than lower-ranked managers about the strategic and operational needs of the organization. And because a manager's rank is usually well known in an organization, it is an effort-conserving way for managers to sort tasks. However, using rank as a signal of how seriously to attend to an issue also has problems, because rank is an imperfect signal of the organizational importance of an issue. Certainly not all the requests of upper-level managers deserve special attention. (In fact, many demands, or perceived interests, of highly ranked managers are taken more seriously than the senders intend.) And certainly, at least some of the initiatives of lower-ranked managers should receive special attention. Self-interest no doubt also explains some of the attentiveness to upper-level managers, which could be an attempt on the part of some managers to ingratiate themselves with those who control resources. Because lower-level managers typically have little resource control, there is not much for a manager to gain personally by giving much attention in their direction.

Setting also plays a signaling role. For example, managers consider large meetings, regardless of what they're about or who called them, to be very important. These meetings also define or interpret "what the organization is about," and they often serve as rituals or ceremonies that keep a sense of community alive in the organization. Because they affirm the place of the individual and others in that community, they are especially important for newcomers and "leaders." Managers probably recognize, if only in some unconscious way, the social significance of these gatherings. Of course, meetings can also be used strategically to legitimize a particular viewpoint or to bolster the position of a particular individual. Whatever the reasons, managers play particularly close attention to what happens in these meetings.

Tasks associated with *external relations*, particularly those associated with resources, also attract serious attention from managers. This is reasonable to some extent. Organizational survival is dependent on the organization's ability to acquire external resources. But, again, there are private benefits for the manager. Being viewed as handling external relations well affects a manager's position of power. There are incentives for managers to engage in these tasks. The data on the managers I studied suggest that external demands may, in fact, unnecessarily divert attention from internal production concerns.

Uncertainty and ambiguity not only are the conditions under which managers carry out their work, they are also the conditions under which the performance of managers is evaluated. I argue that administrative systems, left to their own devices, produce *biased feedback* on the performance of managers. Information on a manager's failings is much more likely to be communicated than information on a manager's successes. Not only are failings more noticeable, partly because they are unexpected, but clients and colleagues have greater incentives to send negative performance reports about a manager than they do to send positive reports. Only the most naive managers are unaware of this.

It should probably not be surprising, given the lack of objective performance standards and, indeed, the likelihood of negatively biased performance reports, that managers get actively involved in managing their reputations in the organization. Indeed, I suggest that this is a major activity for managers and they do it in two ways. First, they regularly send signals to indicate to others that they are smart, well informed, team players with whatever other virtues their particular organization might value, such as competitiveness or cooperativeness. The signals focus on the potential contributions of the managers and on the way they carry out their work: they focus on input and process. For example, the amount of information a manager has stored indicates how valuable that manager is, or how valuable that manager might be if a situation arose where that information were useful. Thus, there are incentives for managers to collect information, probably more information than they "need" to do their job.

It is also in the interest of managers to attend the "right" meetings to show they are responsible and dutiful. They are even better off if the "right" people are at the meetings they attend and the "right" issues, such as external relations, that are important to the organization, are being discussed. They can show how smart they are about matters that others think are important to people who count, particularly those who control resources and can affect a manager's future career. Their attendance at choice meetings can also signal their worth even to, or maybe especially to, those not in attendance. Managers who are invited to the right meetings might be deemed competent simply by association, not because of any real contribution.

In addition to signaling their worth in an active way, managers protect their reputations very carefully. They are generally very reluctant to go out on a limb alone. Because they know the system's feedback on performance is biased, it is often in their interest to share responsibility for actions with others. News about a poor performance will almost undoubtedly get reported. Carrying out their work jointly with other managers protects managers from becoming the "fall guy." By sharing responsibility, they also share the risks.

The above general view gives us some new insights into questions that organizational analysts have repeatedly asked. The first question is: Why are bureaucracies conservative? Part of the explanation—and one that has been offered by a number of analysts—is that organizations become mired in their habits. Procedures are designed on the basis of experience, so they are designed to handle yesterday's problems, not today's. Even if they do identify today's problems accurately, the solutions brought to bear on the problems are likely to be those that are already in place, that is, yesterday's solutions. Thus, behavior controlled by procedures looks backward, rather than forward.

This book suggests another explanation. Bureaucracies are conservative because managers fear failure. Anything not covered by the standard operating procedures of the organization almost always entails risk. Managers have little, if any, experience with nonstandard situations, and there is some chance that things may not turn out well. If they do turn out poorly, it will not go unnoticed. The signaling system is particularly adept at carrying news about failures. Managers cope with this in a couple of ways. Indeed, I suspect managers spend considerable effort making sure they are personally "covered" in the event of adverse outcomes. First, as suggested above, they share their tasks and, therefore, the risks and responsibilities associated with them with other managers, with the result that they engage in high levels of interaction with other managers and tend to react to demands as others make them rather than take the initiative themselves. A second way managers cope is by taking what they write very seriously. They know the written record is fairly permanent and can be used at some later time to reconstruct an event. In contrast, they do not take what they read very seriously. They probably know that when something is put in writing, it is more likely to be something for the record and not anything that has real information value.

This leads to the second question: Why do administrative systems grow? The standard explanation for bureaucratic growth is that managers are greedy for power, prestige, and higher salaries. The explanation developed here argues that administrative growth is likely to occur even with well-intentioned managers who are simply trying to do their job. The managers I studied and the managers that others have studied all worked mainly in a reactive mode and spent a considerable amount of their work time in interactions with others. Most managerial work is oral work for reasons that I discussed in chapter 4. Because there is always uncertainty, a manager's job is mainly to collect and to process information. Because there is always something more to be known, there is no natural limit on managerial interaction. In addition, if managers want to get ahead, the onus is on them to broadcast their competence to others. They cannot count on the system's sensors to recognize their worth. Showing how smart and well-informed they are at meetings is probably the most common way managers do this; they interact a good part of the time with other managers in the same system and often in large group sessions. In chapter 5, I showed that if an additional manager were hired and behaved like other managers on the job — specifically, if he or she initiated interactions and reacted to the demands of others at the same rate — then the demands in the system on other managers would increase, not decrease. The new manager would create more work than he or she would absorb. In this sense, the marginal contribution of the new manager would be negative; but in a system where the value of information cannot be accurately assessed, it is never clear when this point is reached. Consequently, administrative systems grow relatively unchecked by internal efficiency standards. Only when there is some crisis, like a reduction in revenues in the public sector or a loss of a competitive position in the private sector, is an action typically taken to trim management costs.

The third question is about "putting out fires." Why are managers so often caught off guard? A large part of the reason managers are surprised, of course, is that they are working in an environment that is not perfectly predictable. This book suggests another reason. Managerial systems are segmented and information flows are biased. Information that probably should be flowing to the top simply is not getting there. Upper-level managers are ignorant of many of the issues and uncertainties that are percolating below. Upper-level managers keep pretty much to themselves, interacting mainly with each other. They do not seem to put much effort into reaching down into the organization, probably because they do not place a high value on what those in lower levels have to say. And lower-level managers are hesitant to interact with their superiors, especially about matters about which they are uncertain, because they probably fear they would demonstrate their incompetence. The opinions of superiors about their abilities affect their promotion chances. Aspiring lower-level managers no doubt prefer to interact about issues that they have under control.

The perspective taken in this book does not lend itself to simple prescriptions for making administrative systems function better. It does provide an explanation of why managers are continually looking for a formula for success and why books that claim to have such a formula are so popular. Managers work in an environment characterized by uncertainty and ambiguity. What I offer is a complex prescription, perhaps more accurately a framework, based on the premise that the only way to manage an organization successfully is to understand the ambiguities of the environment, the social structure of the system, and the mixed motives of the individuals who make up the organization and determine its behavior.

APPENDIX

The Setting

This study took place in the central office of a large school district whose boundaries encompassed a stable residential area, the central part of a city of one-half million and newly developing middle-class neighborhoods. It served 41,338 elementary and secondary students. Almost 3,000 people were employed by the district; 175 were certified as administrators and 1,800 as teachers and pupil services personnel. Over 1,000 employees were classified: mainly secretarial, food services, and maintenance personnel. The central office, where the study took place, housed 77 administrators, who were responsible in one way or another for managing the business of the district, and 50 nonprofessionals. The rest of the district's personnel were assigned to the schools — thirty-seven elementary schools, six high schools, one vocational center, and one continuation school.

The central office was divided into six major functional areas; the Office of the Superintendent, the Division of Instruction, the Guidance Division, the Office of Adult and Vocational Education, the Personnel and Planning Division, and the Business Office. In addition to the regular school program the district administered a number of special-purpose programs, funded by the state or the federal government for specific purposes or populations. The major programs included both state and federal programs for disadvantaged students and bilingual students, plus a state program for early childhood education.

During the period studied the district was operating pretty much in a "steady state." There was no particular event or set of events that was unusual. Background concerns about resources, desegregation and union negotiations were floating around, but there were no crises or pressing deadlines that seemed to divert attention from day-to-day operations.

The Managers

The managers who participated in the study were all housed in the central office of the school district. Like most education administrators, they all had prior careers as teachers and had spent most of their adult lives as educational professionals. In addition, they were very familiar with the

149

district and with their jobs, having been employed by the district an average of fifteen years. They were also well-educated; 16 percent had training at the B.A. level; 75 percent had master's degrees; and 9 percent had doctorates.

Three hierarchical levels distinguished these managers. Level 1 managers were the highest ranked. They included the superintendent and the associate and assistant superintendents. Level 2 managers were made up of program directors and administrators. Program directors had direct responsibility for the operation of a specific program (for example, the director of the bilingual program); and administrators operated in staff functions (such as labor negotiations) and reported directly to the superintendent. Level 3 managers were supervisors who mainly carried out liaison activities with the schools. They reported to Level 2 managers.

Data Collection

Prior to recording the data at random signals, managers completed a brief questionnaire in which they gave information on themselves, such as education, sex, number of years in the district, length of time in present position, and salary. They also provided a list of individuals or groups (e.g., teachers) with whom they worked most. This list provided the basis of the initiator question in the random activity questionnaire. In a few cases a name was added or changed on the random activity questionnaire during the first two days of data collection, but generally the list they provided worked quite well. I was able to identify the source of 85 percent of the work activity managers reported. The remainder fell into the category "other."

Every day during which data were collected, I was on-site to ensure quality control and to keep individual managers involved in the data collection effort. One thing I particularly stressed during this time was the importance of responding to the random "beep" as it occurred so that the observations would be truly representative of their work behavior. I also used this time to observe in an unstructured way the general comings and goings of the office so that I would be aware of any events that might disrupt normal operations. Fortunately, there were none. Data were collected over a six-week period beginning in October and ending in early December. This avoided the September start-up period for the school district as well as any wind-down that might have occurred before Christmas break.

The final participation rate in the study was very good. Data from fifty-two of the seventy-seven managers were good enough to include in the analyses. Six administrators were not interested in participating from the outset. Because there were no sanctions and because the data collection was somewhat burdensome, it is surprising that more managers did not opt out.

The managers that chose not to participate explained that they simply did not want to be bothered with data collection and that they were not particularly interested in the study results. There was no attempt to persuade them to participate. If reluctant managers felt pushed into cooperation, I feared the quality of their reporting would suffer. Because full monitoring was impossible, the study was heavily dependent on the integrity of the data as reported by managers.

In addition to the six managers who declined to participate from the start, the occupants of three positions filled midway through the study were not included. Data from an additional sixteen managers were not included because their data did not meet quality and/or quantity criteria. Only managers who completed at least two full weeks of data collection and were responsive to the random signals as they occurred were included in the analysis.

The distribution according to length of participation of the fifty-two managers who were included in the analyses was as follows:

TABLE A.1 Number of Respondents by Length of Participation
Weeks of Data Collected

	2	2-3	3-4	4-5	5-6	Total
Managers	5	5	11	19	12	52

The fifty-two managers were pretty well distributed across divisions in the system, and the participation rates of the divisions were fairly high. (See Table A.2.) The main exception was in the Division of Guidance. Data on only nine of the twenty-one administrators were included in the analysis. Four persons declined to participate; seven had insufficient data; and one person was hired after the study was underway. This lower level of participation can be explained partially by the office layout in the division. The desks of most of these administrators were together in one large area, so lack of cooperation may have been contagious.

The final sample was also distributed pretty well across hierarchic levels, as shown in Table A.3.

TABLE A.2   Participation Within Divisions

Division	Number of Managers	Number of Participants	Participation Rate
Superintendent's Office	5	5	1.00
Division of Instruction	28	18	.64
Division of Personnel/Planning	6	6	1.00
Business and Data Processing	4	3	.75
Division of Guidance	21	9	.42
Division of Adult/Vocational Education	12	10	.83
Health Services	1	1	1.00
Total	77	52	.68

TABLE A.3   Participation Across Levels

Level of Managers	Number of Participants	Number Whose Data Were Used	Participation Rate
1	5	4	.80
2	17	15	.88
3	55	33	.60
Total	77	52	.68

REFERENCES

Ahlbrandt, R. S. "Efficiency in the Provision Fire Services." *Public Choice*, 1973, 19:1–42.

Akerlof, George, and W. T. Dickens. "The Economic Consequences of Cognitive Dissonance." *American Economic Review*, 1982, 72:307–19.

Aldrich, Howard E. *Organizations and Environments*. Englewood Cliffs, N.J.: Prentice-Hall, 1979.

Allen, T. J. and S. I. Cohen. "Information Flow in Research and Development Laboratories." *Administrative Science Quarterly*, 1969, 14:12–19.

Allison, Graham T. *The Essence of Decision: Explaining the Cuban Missile Crisis*. Boston: Little, Brown, 1971.

Allison, Graham T., and M. H. Halperin. "Bureaucratic Politics: Paradigm and Some Policy Implications." In R. Tanter and R. H. Ullman (eds.), *Theory and Policy in International Relations*. Princeton: Princeton University Press, 1972.

Alter, J., P. Abramson, and V. Coppola. "Tickets to the Stars." *Newsweek*, July 9, 1984, pp. 48–49.

Aronson, E., M. Brewer, and J. M. Carlsmith. "Experimentation in Social Psychology." In G. Lindszey and E. Aronson (eds.), *Handbook of Social Psychology*, 2nd ed. Reading, Mass.: Addison-Wesley, 1968.

Arrow, Kenneth. *The Limits of Organization*. New York: Norton, 1974.

Barnard, Chester I. *The Functions of the Executive*. Cambridge: Harvard University Press, 1962.

Barlund, S. C., and C. Harland. "Propinquity and Prestige as Determinants of Communication Networks." *Sociometry*, 1964, 26:466–79.

Baumol, William. *Business Behavior, Value, and Growth*. New York: Macmillan, 1959.

Bear, G., and A. Hodun. "Implicational Principles and the Cognition of Confirmatory, Contradictory, Incomplete, and Irrelevant Information." *Journal of Personality and Social Psychology*, 1975, 32:594–604.

Bennis, Warren. "Why Leaders Can't Lead." In Rosabeth Moss Kanter and Barry A. Stein (eds.), *Life in Organizations*. New York: Basic Books, 1979.

153

Berle, A. A. and G. C. Means. *The Modern Corporation and Private Property*. New York: Commerce Clearing House, 1932.

Blau, Peter M. *The Dynamics of Bureaucracy*, 2nd ed. Chicago: University of Chicago Press, 1963.

———. 'A Formal Theory of Differentiation in Organizations." *American Sociological Review*, 1970, 35:201–18.

Burns, James McGregor. *Leadership*. New York: Harper & Row, 1978.

Burns, T. "The Direction of Activity and Communication in a Departmental Executive Group." *Human Relations*, 1954, 7:73–97.

———. "Management in Action." *Operational Research Quarterly*, 1957, 8:45–60.

Campbell, John P. *Managerial Behavior, Performance, and Effectiveness*. New York: McGraw-Hill, 1970.

Carlson, S. *Executive Behavior: A Study of the Workload and the Working Methods of Managing Directors*. Stockholm: Strombergs, 1951.

Carroll, Stephen J., and Dennis J. Gillen. "Are the Classical Management Functions Useful in Describing Managerial Work?" *Academy of Management Review*, 1987, 12:38–51.

Casey, Hanoria. "Management Behavior." Ph.D. diss., School of Education, Stanford University, 1980.

Child, John. "Organizational Structure, Environment, and Performance: The Role of Strategic Choice." *Sociology*, 1972, 6:2–22.

Cohen, Michael D., and James G. March. *Leadership and Ambiguity: The American College President*. New York: McGraw-Hill, 1974.

Cohen, Michael D., James G. March, and Johan P. Olsen. "A Garbage Can Model of Organizational Choice." *Administrative Science Quarterly*, 1972, 17:1–25.

Collins, Randall. "On the Microfoundations of Macrosociology." *American Journal of Sociology*, 1981, 86:984–1014.

Connolly, Terry. "Information Processing and Decisionmaking in Organizations." In B. Staw and G. Salancik (eds.), *New Directions in Organization Behavior*. Chicago: St. Clair, 1977, pp. 205–34.

Crozier, Michel. *The Bureaucratic Phenomenon*. Chicago: University of Chicago Press, 1964.

Cyert, Richard, and James G. March. *A Behavioral Theory of the Firm*. Englewood Cliffs, N.J.: Prentice-Hall, 1963.

Dalton, M. *Men Who Manage*. New York: John Wiley, 1959.

Dearborn, DeWitt, and G. A. Simon. "Selective Perception." *Sociometry*, 1958, 21:140–43.

De Lorean, John Z. *On a Clear Day You Can See General Motors*. Grosse Pointe, Mich.: Wright Enterprises, 1979.

DiMaggio, Paul J., and Walter W. Powell. "The Iron Cage Revisited: Institutional Isomorphism and Collective Rationality in Organizational Fields." *American Sociological Review*, 1983, 48:147–60.

Dornbusch, Sanford M., and W. Richard Scott. *Evaluation and the Exercise of Authority: A Theory of Control Applied to Diverse Organizations*. San Francisco: Jossey-Bass, 1975.

Downs, Anthony. *Inside Bureaucracy*. Boston: Little, Brown, 1967.

Dubin, R., and S. L. Spray. "Executive Behavior and Interaction." *Industrial Relations*, 1964, 3:99–108.

Einhorn, H. J., and R. M. Hogarth. "Behavioral Decision Theory: Processes of Judgment and Choice." *Annual Review of Psychology*, 1981, 32:53–88.

El Sawy, Omar A. "Temporal Perspectives and Managerial Attention: A Study of Chief Executives' Strategic Behavior." Ph.D. diss., Graduate School of Business, Stanford University, 1983.

Feldman, Martha J., and James G. March. "Information in Organizations as Signal and Symbol." *Administrative Science Quarterly*, 1981, 26:171–86.

Festinger, Leon. "Informal Social Communication." *Psychological Review*, 1950, 57:271–82.

———. "A Theory of Social Comparison Processes." *Human Relations*, 1954, 7:117–40.

Fiske, Susan T. "Attention and Weight in Person Perception: The Impact of Negative and Extreme Behavior." *Journal of Personality and Social Psychology*, 1980, 38:889–906.

Fiske, Susan T., and Shelley E. Taylor. *Social Cognition*. Reading, Mass.: Addison-Wesley, 1984.

Frank, Robert H. *Choosing the Right Pond: Human Behavior and the Quest for Status*. New York: Oxford University Press, 1985.

Galbraith, Jay. *Organization Design*. Reading, Mass.: Addison-Wesley, 1977.

Geneen, Harold. *Managing*. Garden City, N.Y.: Doubleday, 1984.

Glauser, Michael. "Upward Information Flow in Organizations: Review and Conceptual Analysis." *Human Relations*, 1984, 37:613–43.

Granovetter, Mark. "The Strength of Weak Ties." *American Journal of Sociology*, 1973, 78:1360–80.

Greenwald, A. G. "Self and Memory." In G. H. Bower (ed.), *The Psychology of Learning and Motivation*. New York: Academic Press, 1981.

Greenwald, A. G., and C. Leavitt. "Audience Involvement in Advertising: Four Levels." *Journal of Consumer Research*, 1984, 11:581–92.

Hall, Richard H. *Organizations: Structure and Process*. New York: Prentice-Hall, 1972.

Halperin, M. H. *Bureaucratic Politics and Foreign Policy*. Washington, D.C.: The Brookings Institution, 1974.

Hannan, Michael T., and John Freeman. "The Internal Politics of Growth and Decline." In Meyer and Associates (eds.), *Studies on Environment and Organization*. San Francisco: Jossey-Bass, 1978.

Hannaway, Jane. "Administrative Costs and Administrative Behavior Associated with Categorical Programs." *Educational Evaluation and Policy Analysis*, 1985a, 7:57–64.

_____. "Managerial Behavior, Uncertainty, and Hierarchy: Notes Toward a Synthesis." *Human Relations*, 1985b, 38:1085–1100.

_____. "Supply Creates Demands: An Organizational Process View of Administrative Expansion." *Journal of Policy Analysis and Management*, 1987, 7:118–34.

Harper, W. K. "Executive Time: A Corporation's Most Valuable, Scarce, and Irrecoverable Resource." D.B.A. thesis, Harvard University, 1968.

Harrell, Thomas W. and Margaret S. "Stanford MBA Careers: A 20-year-Longitudinal Study." Research Paper No. 723. Graduate School of Business, Stanford University, 1984.

Hastings, Anne. "Shipping the Strings: Local and State Administrators Discuss Chapter 2." *Phi Delta Kappa*, 1983, 65:194–98.

Hemphill, J. K. "Job Descriptions for Executives." *Harvard Business Review*, 1959, 37:55–67.

_____. "Dimensions of Executive Positions." Research Monograph Number 98. Columbus: Ohio State University, Bureau of Business Research, 1960.

Hickson, Donald L., et al. "A 'Strategic Contingencies' Theory of Intraorganizational Power." *Administrative Science Quarterly*, 1971, 16:216–29.

Hirsch, Fred. *The Social Limits to Growth*. Cambridge: Harvard University Press, 1976.

Homans, George. *The Human Group*. New York: Harcourt, Brace and World, 1950.

Horne, J. H., and Tom Lupton. "The Work Activities of 'Middle' Managers – An Exploratory Study." *The Journal of Management Studies*, 1965, 2:14–33.

Isen, A. M. and Hastorf, A. H. (eds.). *Cognitive Social Psychology*. New York: Elsevier/North Holland, 1982.

Iacocca, Lee. 1984.

Janis, Irving L. *Victims of Groupthink*. Boston: Houghton Mifflin, 1972.

Janis, Irving L., and Leon Mann. *Decision Making*. New York: The Free Press, 1977.

Kahneman, Daniel, and Amos Tversky. "Choices, Values, and Frames." *American Psychologist*, 1984, 39:341–50.

_____. "Prospect Theory: An Analysis of Decisions Under Risk." *Econometrica*, 1979, 47:263–91.

Kahneman, D., P. Slovic, and A. Tversky. *Judgment Under Uncertainty: Heuristics and Biases*. Cambridge: Cambridge University Press, 1982.

Kanter, Rosabeth Moss, and Barry Stein (eds.). *Life in Organizations*. New York: Basic Books, 1979.

Kelly, J. "The Study of Executive Behavior by Activity Sampling." *Human Relations*, 1964, 17:277–87.

Kiesler, Charles A. and Sara B. *Conformity*. Reading Mass.: Addison-Wesley, 1969.

Kiesler, Charles A., B. E. Collins, and N. Miller. "Attitude Change: A Critical Analysis of Theoretical Approaches." New York: John Wiley, 1969.

Kiesler, Sara, and Lee Sproull. "Managerial Response to Changing Environments: Perspectives on Problem Sensing from Social Cognition." *Administrative Science Quarterly*, 1982, 27:548–70.

Kolarska, Lena, and Howard Aldrich. "Exit, Voice and Silence: Consumers' and Managers' Responses to Organizational Decline." *Organization Studies*, 1980, 1:41–58.

Koopmans, Tjalling. *Three Essays on the State of Economic Science*. New York: McGraw-Hill, 1957.

Kotter, John P. *The General Managers*. New York: The Free Press, 1982.

Lawler, E. E., L. W. Porter, and A. Tennenbaum. "A Manager's Attitudes Toward Interaction Episodes." *Journal of Applied Psychology*, 1968, 52:432–39.

Leavitt, Harold J. "Effects of Certain Communication Patterns on Group Performance." *Journal of Abnormal and Social Psychology*, 151, 46:38–50.

Lichtenstein, Sara, and P. Slovic. "Reversal of Preferences Between Bids and Choices in Gambling Decisions." *Journal of Experimental Psychology*, 1971, 89:46–55.

Lieberson, Stanley, and James F. O'Connor. "Leadership and Organizational Performance: A Study of Large Corporations." *American Sociological Review*, 1972, 37:117–30.

MacKenzie, R. Alec. *The Time Trap*. New York: McGraw-Hill, 1972.

Mahoney, T. A., J. H. Jerdee, and S. J. Carroll. *Development of Managerial Performance: A Research Approach*. Cincinnati, Ohio: Southwestern, 1963.

March, James G. "The Business Firm as a Political Coalition." *Journal of Politics*, 1962, 24:662–78.

———. "Model Bias in Social Action." *Review of Educational Research*, 1973, 42:413–29.

———. "Bounded Rationality, Ambiguity, and the Engineering of Choice." *Bell Journal of Economics*, 1978, 9:587–608.

———. "Footnotes to Organizational Change." *Administrative Science Quarterly*, 1981, 26:563–77.

March, James G., and Martha Feldman. "Information in Organizations as Signal and Symbol." *Administrative Science Quarterly*, 1981, 26:171–86.

March, James G. and James C. "Performance Sampling in Social Matches." *Administrative Science Quarterly*, 1978, 23:434–53.

March, James G., and Johan P. Olsen. "Organizational Learning and the Ambiguity of the Past." In J. G. March and J. P. Olsen (eds.), *Ambiguity and Choices in Organizations*. Bergen: Universitetsforlaget, 1976, pp. 54–68.

March, James G., and Guje Sevón. "Gossip, Information, and Decision Making." In L. S. Sproull and P. S. Larkey (eds.). *Advances in Information Processing in Organizations*, vol 1. Greenwich, Conn.: JAI Press, 1984.

March, James G., and Zur Shapiro. "Behavioral Decision Theory and Organizational Decision Theory." In G. R. Ungson and D. N. Braunstein (eds.), *Decision Making: An Interdisciplinary Inquiry*. Boston: Kent, 1982.

March, James G., and Herbert A. Simon. *Organizations*. New York: John Wiley, 1958.

Marris, Robin. *The Economic Theory of Managerial Capitalism*. London: Macmillan, 1966.

Mayhew, Bruce. "Structuralism versus Individualism: Part I, Shadowboxing in the Dark." *Social Forces*, 1980, 59:335–75.

———. "Structuralism versus Individualism: Part II, Ideological and Other Obfuscations." *Social Forces*, 1981, 59:627–48.

Mechanic, David. "Sources of Power of Lower Participants in Complex Organizations." *Administrative Science Quarterly*, 1962, 7:349–64.

Merton, Robert. *Social Theory and Social Structure*. New York: The Free Press, 1968.

Meyer, John, and Brian Rowan. "Institutionalized Organizations: Formal Structure as Myth and Ceremony." *American Journal of Sociology*, 1977, 83:340–63.

Meyer, John, and W. Richard Scott. *Organizational Environments: Ritual and Rationality*. Beverly Hills, Calif.: Sage, 1983.

Migue, J. L., and G. Belanger. "Towards a General Theory of Managerial Discretion." *Public Choice*, 1974, 17:27–43.

Miller, Gary J., and Terry M. Moe. "Bureaucrats, Legislators, and the Size of Government." *American Political Science Review*, 1983, 77:297–322.

Miner, J. B. *Management Theory*. New York: Macmillan, 1971.

———. *Theories of Organizational Structure and Process*. Chicago: Dryden, 1982.

Mintzberg, Henry. *The Nature of Managerial Work*. New York: Harper & Row, 1973.

———. "An Emerging Strategy of 'Direct' Research." *Administrative Science Quarterly*, 1979, 24:582–89.

Mintzberg, Henry, Duru Raisinghani, and André Theoret. "The Structure of Unstructured Decision Processes." *Administrative Science Quarterly*, 1976, 21:246–75.

Nisbett, Richard, and Lee Ross. *Human Inference*. New York: John Wiley, 1980.

Niskanen, William A. *Bureaucracy and Representative Government*. Chicago: Aldine, Atherton, 1971.

———. "Bureaucrats and Politicians." *Journal of Law and Economics*, 1975, 18:617.

O'Reilly, Charles A. "The Use of Information in Organizational Decision Making: A Model and Some Propositions." In L. L. Cummings and Barry M. Staw. (eds.), *Research in Organizational Behavior*, vol. 5. Greenwich, Conn.: JAI Press, 1983, pp. 103–40.

O'Reilly, Charles A., J. Chatman, and J. Anderson. "Message Flow and Decision Making." In L. Porter et al. (eds.), *Handbook of Organizational Communication*. New York: Sage, 1987.

O'Reilly, Charles A., and Karlene H. Roberts. "Failures in Upward Communication in Organizations: Three Possible Culprits." Berkeley: Institute of Industrial Relations, University of California, 1973.

Ouchi, William G. "Markets, Bureaucracies, and Clans." *Administrative Science Quarterly*, 1980, 25:129–41.

Parducci, A. "The Relativism of Absolute Judgments." *Scientific American*, 1968, 219:84–90.

Parkinson, Cyril Northcote. *Parkinson's Law and Other Studies of Administration*. Boston: Houghton Mifflin, 1957.

Peters, Thomas J., and Nancy Austin. *A Passion for Excellence: The Leadership Difference*. New York: Random House, 1985.

Peters, Thomas J., and Robert H. Waterman, Jr. *In Search of Excellence: Lessons from America's Best-Run Companies*. New York: Harper & Row, 1982.

Peterson, Penelope. "Direct Instruction Reconsidered." In P. L. Peterson and H. J. Walberg (eds.), *Research on Teaching: Concepts, Findings, and Implications*. Berkeley, Calif.: McCutchan, 1979, pp. 57–69.

Pfeffer, Jeffrey. "The Ambiguity of Leadership." *Academy of Management Review*, 1977, 2:104–12.

———. *Power in Organizations*. Boston: Pitman, 1981.

160   REFERENCES

Pfeffer, Jeffrey, and Gerald R. Salancik. *The External Control of Organizations: A Resource Dependence Perspective*. New York: Harper & Row, 1978.

Pfeffer, Jeffrey, G. R. Salancik, and H. Leblebici. "The Effect of Uncertainty on the Use of Social Influence in Organizational Decision Making." *Administrative Science Quarterly*, 1976, 21:227–45.

Pounds, W. "The Process of Problem Finding." *Industrial Management Review [Sloan Management Review]*, 1969, 11:1–19.

Radner, Roy, and Michael Rothschild. "Notes on the Allocation of Effort." *Journal of Economic Theory*, 1975, 10:358–76.

Roberts, David R. *Executive Compensation*. Glencoe, Ill.: The Free Press, 1959.

Rosenshine, B. "Content, Time and Direct Instruction." In P. Peterson and H. Walberg (eds.), *Research on Teaching: Concepts, Findings, and Implications*. Berkeley, Calif.: McCutchan, 1979.

Salancik, Gerald R., and Jeffrey Pfeffer. "Constraints on Administrator Discretion: The Limited Influence of Mayors on City Budgets." *Urban Affairs Quarterly*, 1977, 12:475–98.

_____. "A Social Information Processing Approach to Job Attitudes and Task Design." *Administrative Science Quarterly*, 1978, 23:224–53.

Sarnoff, I., and P. G. Zimbardo. "Anxiety, Fear and Social Affiliation." *Journal of Abnormal and Social Psychology*, 1961, 62:356–63.

Savas, E. S. "Solid Waste Collection in Metropolitan Areas." In E. Ostrom (ed.), *The Delivery of Urban Services*. Beverly Hills, Calif: Sage, 1976.

Sayles, Leonard R. *Managerial Behavior*. New York: McGraw-Hill, 1964.

Schachter, Stanley. *The Psychology of Affiliation: Experimental Studies of the Source of Gregariousness*. Stanford: Stanford University Press, 1959.

Scott, W. Richard. "Organizational Structure." *Annual Review of Sociology*, 1975, 1:1–20.

_____. *Organizations: Rational, Natural, and Open Systems*. Englewood Cliffs, N.J.: Prentice-Hall, 1981.

Selten, Reinhold. "Elementary Theory of Slack-Ridden Competition." In J. E. Stiglitz and F. Mathewson (eds.), *New Developments in the Theory of Market Structure*. New York: Macmillan, 1985.

Shartle, C. L. *Executive Performance and Leadership*. Englewood Cliffs, N.J.: Prentice-Hall, 1956.

Sherif, Muzafer, and C. I. Horland. *Social Judgment: Assimilation and Contrast Effects in Communication and Attitude Change*. New Haven: Yale University Press, 1961.

Sherman, Stratford. "'Why the Youngsters' Party May Be Ending." *Fortune*, November 24, 1986, pp. 29–40.

Shoemaker, J., and H. W. Fraser. "What Principals Can Do: Some Implications from Studies of Effective Schooling." *Phi Delta Kappa*, 1981, 63:178–82.

Simon, Herbert A. *The Shape of Automation*. New York: Macmillan, 1965.

_____. "A Behavioral Model of Rational Choice." *Quarterly Journal of Economics*, 1955, 69:99–118. Reprinted in H. A. Simon, *Models of Bounded Rationality*, vol. 2. Cambridge, Mass: MIT Press. 1982, chap 7.2.

_____. *Administrative Behavior*. 2nd ed. New York: The Free Press, 1976.

_____. "On the Concept of Organizational Goal." *Administrative Science Quarterly*, 1964, 9:1–22.

_____. "Rational Decision Making in Business Organizations." *American Economic Review*, 1979, 69:493–513.

_____. "Human Nature in Politics: The Dialogue of Psychology with Political Science." *American Political Science Review*, 1985, 79:293–304.

Slovic, Paul, and S. Lichtenstein. "Preference Reversals: A Broader Perspective." *American Economic Review*, 1983, 73:596–603.

Slovic, Paul, B. Fischoff, and S. Lichtenstein. "Behavioral Decision Theory." *Annual Review of Psychology*, 1977, 28:1–39.

_____. "Facts versus Fears: Understanding Perceived Risk." In Daniel Kahneman, Paul Slovic, and Amos Tversky (eds.), *Judgment Under Uncertainty: Heuristics and Biases*. Cambridge: Cambridge University Press, 1982, pp. 463–89.

Snyder, M., and W. Swann. "Hypothesis-Testing Processes in Social Interaction." *Journal of Personality and Social Psychology*, 1978, 36:1202–12.

Spence, A. Michael. *Market Signalling*. Cambridge: Harvard University Press, 1974.

Sproull, Lee S. "Beliefs in Organizations." In Paul C. Nystrom and William H. Starbuck (eds.), *Handbook of Organizational Design*, vol. 2. New York: Oxford University Press, 1981.

_____. "The Nature of Managerial Attention." In L. S. Sproull (ed.), *Advances in Information Processing in Organizations*. Greenwich, Conn.: JAI Press, 1984.

Sproull, Lee S., S. S. Weiner, and D. B. Wolf. *Organizing an Anarchy*. Chicago: University of Chicago Press, 1978.

Staaf, Robert. "The Public School System in Transition." In T. E. Bocherding (ed.), *Budgets and Bureaucrats: The Sources of Government Growth*. Durham: Duke University Press, 1977.

Starbuck, William H. "Organizational Growth and Development." In James G. March (ed.), *Handbook of Organizations*. Chicago: Rand McNally, 1965.

Steinbrunner, John D. *The Cybernetic Theory of Decision*. Princeton: Princeton University Press, 1974.

Stewart, Rosemary. "The Use of Diaries to Study Managers' Jobs." *Journal of Management Studies*, 1965, 2:228-35.

———. *Managers and Their Jobs*. London: Macmillan, 1967.

———. *Choices for the Manager*. Englewood Cliffs, N.J.: Prentice-Hall, 1982.

Stogdill, R. M., et al. "Patterns of Administrative Performance." Research Monograph Number 81. Columbus, Ohio: Ohio State University, Bureau of Business Research, 1956.

Taubman, Philip. "At State, Dissent Gives Rise to Praise." *New York Times*, November 8, 1982, p. 12.

Teichman, Yona. "Predisposition for Anxiety and Affiliation." *Journal of Personality and Social Psychology*, 1974, 29:405-10.

Thompson, James D. *Organizations in Action*. New York: McGraw-Hill, 1967.

Thompson, James S., and A. Tuden. "Strategies, Structures and Processes of Organizational Decision." In J. D. Thompson et al. (eds.), *Comparative Studies in Administration*. Pittsburgh: University of Pittsburgh Press, 1959, pp. 195-216.

Thompson, V. A. *Modern Organization*. New York: Knopf, 1961.

Tullock, Gordon. *The Politics of Bureaucracy*. Washington, D.C.: Public Affairs Press, 1965.

Tversky, Amos, and D. Kahneman. "Availability: A Heuristic for Judging Frequency and Probability." *Cognitive Psychology*, 1973, 5:207-32.

———. "Judgment Under Uncertainty: Heuristics and Biases." *Science*, 1974, 1124-31.

———. "The Framing of Decisions and the Psychology of Choice." *Science*, 1981, 211:453-58.

Ungson, G. R., D. W. Braustein, and P. D. Hall. "Managerial Information Processing: A Research Review." *Administrative Science Quarterly*, 1981, 26:116-34.

Warwick, Donald P. *A Theory of Public Bureaucracy: Politics, Personality, and Organization in the State Department*. Cambridge: Harvard University Press, 1975.

Webb, Eugene, et al. *Unobtrusive Measures: Nonreactive Research in the Social Sciences.* New York: Rand McNally, 1966.

Webb, Eugene, and Karl Weick. "Unobtrusive Measures in Organizational Theory: A Reminder." *Administrative Science Quarterly*, 1979, 24:650–59.

Weber, Max. *Theory of Social and Economic Organization.* New York: Free Press, 1947.

Weick, Karl E. "Educational Organizations as Loosely Coupled Systems." *Administrative Science Quarterly*, 1976, 21:1–19.

―――. "Cognitive Processes in Organizations." In Barry M. Staw (ed.), *Research in Organizational Behavior*, vol. 1, Greenwich, Conn.: JAI Press, 1979, pp. 41–74.

Weimer, David L., and C. Lawrence Evans. "Communication on Miller and Moe's 'Bureaucrats, Legislators, and the Size of Government.'" February 1985. Mimeographed.

"Who's Excellent Now?" *Business Week*, November 5, 1984, pp. 76–88.

Wilensky, H. L. *Organizational Intelligence.* New York: Basic Books, 1967.

Williamson, Oliver E. *The Economics of Discretionary Behavior: Managerial Objectives in a Theory of the Firm.* New York: Prentice-Hall, 1964.

―――. *Markets and Hierarchies: Analysis and Antitrust Implications.* New York: The Free Press, 1975.

―――. *The Economic Institutions of Capitalism.* New York: The Free Press, 1985.

Wirdenius, H. *Supervisors at Work.* Stockholm: The Swedish Council for Personnel Administration. 1958.

Wolcott, Harry F. *The Man in the Principal's Office: An Ethnography.* New York: Holt, Rinehart and Winston, 1973.

Zelditch, Morris. "Can You Really Study an Army in the Laboratory?" In Amaitar Elzioni (ed.), *A Sociological Reader on Complex Organizations*. 2nd ed. New York: Holt, Rinehart and Winston, 1969, pp. 528–39.

Zimbardo, P. G. *The Cognitive Control of Motivation: The Consequences of Choice and Dissonance.* Glenview, Ill.: Scott-Foresman, 1969.

Zimbardo, P. G., and R. Formica. "Emotional Comparison and Self-Esteem as Determinants of Affiliation." *Journal of Personality*, 1963, 31:141–62.

INDEX